THE SEARCHERS

THE
SEARCHERS

A Quest for Faith in the Valley of Doubt

JOSEPH LOCONTE

THOMAS NELSON
Since 1798

NASHVILLE   DALLAS   MEXICO CITY   RIO DE JANEIRO

Published in Nashville, Tennessee, by Thomas Nelson. Thomas Nelson is a registered trademark of Thomas Nelson, Inc.

Author is represented by the literary agency of Alive Communications, Inc., 7680 Goddard Street, Suite 200, Colorado Springs, CO 80920, www.alivecommunications.com.

Thomas Nelson, Inc., titles may be purchased in bulk for educational, business, fund-raising, or sales promotional use. For information, please e-mail SpecialMarkets@ThomasNelson.com.

Unless otherwise noted, Scripture quotations are taken from THE HOLY BIBLE, NEW INTERNATIONAL VERSION®, NIV®. Copyright © 1973, 1978, 1984, 2011 by Biblica, Inc.™ Used by permission of Zondervan. All rights reserved worldwide. www.zondervan.com.

Scripture quotations marked NKJV are taken from THE NEW KING JAMES VERSION. © 1982 by Thomas Nelson, Inc. Used by permission. All rights reserved.

ISBN 978-1-40027-482-6 (IE)

Library of Congress Cataloging-in-Publication Data

Loconte, Joe, 1961-
The searchers : a quest for faith in the valley of doubt / Joseph Loconte.
    p. cm.
Includes bibliographical references.
ISBN 978-1-59555-446-8
1. Bible. N.T. Luke XXIV, 13-35--Criticism, interpretation, etc. 2. Jesus Christ--Appearances. 3. Faith. I. Title.
BS2595.52.L63 2012
226.4'06--dc23

2011050532

Printed in the United States of America

12 13 14 15 16 QG 6 5 4 3 2 1

For Mom and Dad
For my grandparents,
Giuseppe and Esther Aiello and
Michele and Theodora Loconte,
and for the children of Ventotene

If I can get to the celestial city, I am sure to be in safety there: I must venture.

—John Bunyan, *The Pilgrim's Progress*

The sweetest thing in all my life has been the longing—
to reach the Mountain, to find the place where all
the beauty came from . . . Do you think it all meant
nothing, all the longing? The longing for home?

—C. S. Lewis, *Till We Have Faces*

Contents

Preface

A Conversation on the Road to Emmaus

In the area of Palestine, during the period when Rome was transforming itself from a republic into an empire, charismatic religious leaders might arise to challenge imperial rule. Their campaigns inevitably ended the same way: arrest, trial, and swift execution. Such appeared to be the case with a Jewish leader known as Jesus of Nazareth. After an immensely successful public career that lasted until about AD 33, he was seized in the city of Jerusalem and crucified by the Romans on the charge of sedition.

Just days after his execution, two of his followers fled the scene to seek sanctuary in their hometown of Emmaus, not far from Jerusalem. Along the way they encountered another traveler, a stranger, who seemed unaware of the deadly turn of events in Jerusalem. A portion of their conversation has come down to us through the writings of a Gentile, most likely the author known as Luke. A physician by trade, Luke was a careful chronicler of the early Jesus movement. His record of events—based in part on the recollection of eyewitnesses—is widely recognized for its historical precision and accuracy. The following passage is Luke's account of their provocative conversation.

Now that same day two of them were going to a village called Emmaus, about seven miles from Jerusalem. They were talking with each other about everything that had happened. As they talked and discussed these things with each other, Jesus himself came up and walked along with them; but they were kept from recognizing him.

He asked them, "What are you discussing together as you walk along?"

They stood still, their faces downcast. One of them, named Cleopas, asked him, "Are you only a visitor to Jerusalem and do not know the things that have happened there in these days?"

"What things?" he asked.

"About Jesus of Nazareth," they replied. "He was a prophet, powerful in word and deed before God and all the people. The chief priests and our rulers handed him over to be sentenced to death, and they crucified him; but we had hoped that he was the one who was going to redeem Israel. And what is more, it is the third day since all this took place. In addition, some of our women amazed us. They went to the tomb early this morning but didn't find his body. They came and told us that they had seen a vision of angels, who said he was alive. Then some of our companions went to the tomb and found it just as the women had said, but him they did not see."

He said to them, "How foolish you are, and how slow of heart to believe all that the prophets have spoken! Did not the Christ have to suffer these things and then enter his glory?" And beginning with Moses and all the Prophets, he explained to them what was said in all the Scriptures concerning himself.

As they approached the village to which they were going, Jesus acted as if he were going farther. But they urged him strongly, "Stay with us, for it is nearly evening; the day is almost over." So he went in to stay with them.

When he was at the table with them, he took bread, gave thanks, broke it and began to give it to them. Then their eyes were opened and they recognized him, and he disappeared from their sight. They asked each other, "Were not our hearts burning within us while he talked with us on the road and opened the Scriptures to us?"

They got up and returned at once to Jerusalem. There they found the Eleven and those with them, assembled together and saying, "It is true! The Lord has risen and has appeared to Simon!" Then the two told what had happened on the way, and how Jesus was recognized by them when he broke the bread.

Luke 24:13–35

Introduction

Two Friends on a Quest

"Now that same day two of them were going
to a village called Emmaus, about seven
miles from Jerusalem. They were talking
with each other about everything that had
happened."

——◆——

In Andrei Kravchuk's 2005 film The Italian, *we are introduced to a six-
year-old abandoned boy, Vanya Solntsev, who must endure the severities
and injustices of a thoroughly bleak institution, a Russian orphanage.
One day a wealthy Italian couple arrives, eager to adopt a child. They
choose Vanya and make plans to take him back to their villa in Italy.
To Vanya's fellow inmates, it is an impossible dream come true: to leave
what seems like an endless winter of existence and escape to Italy—to
Italy!—where the warm sun rises over fields of grapes and olives and figs.
To be among families who share their food and affection in abundance.
Vanya's friends, out of envy, give him a nickname: the Italian.*

*Then Vanya discovers his mother is still alive. He secretly teaches himself
to read so he can learn her address from his personal files. Vanya does not want*

to live with the lovely family in lovely Italy. He wants to find his mother because somehow he knows that's where his home is. So he escapes from the orphanage and sneaks on board a commuter train to her city. Pursued relentlessly by corrupt staff and police, Vanya refuses to give up hope.

The irresistible claim in The Italian *is the idea of "home" as a place where we experience our deepest sense of belonging, meaning, and love. This little boy will risk everything to find it. Inspired by actual events, the film closes with Vanya reunited with his mother. After a time, he writes his friend Anton, recently adopted by the Italian couple in his place.*

"Hello Anton," he writes. "Thank you for your letter. I didn't know oranges grow where you live. Here it rains all the time, but it's warm inside."

Tucked away in the pages of the Bible is a tale of two friends, a stranger, and a desperate quest for faith in a world gone mad with doubt.

The companions are men on the run, fugitives from the authorities in Jerusalem. Their destination is a village called Emmaus, a short distance from the Holy City. The violent events of the last few days have nearly overwhelmed them. These men need a safe haven, a place to make sense of what has just happened in their lives: they are going home.[1] Indifferent to the sky or earth around them, they are absorbed in conversation. They argue. They interrupt one another. They fall silent—and then go at it again.[2]

The subject of their disagreement is the execution of a controversial teacher and faith healer in Jerusalem. He was known as Jesus, a carpenter's son from Nazareth, and a Jew. Many among the Jews believed he was a prophet, a spokesman for God. Some dismissed him as a huckster, others as a rabble-rouser. These friends thought he might be Israel's best hope for political liberation. They both counted themselves among his followers.

Many others, of course, would do the same in the years and centuries after his death. Indeed, no figure in history has inspired such a wealth and diversity of music, literature, and art. The Dutch painter Rembrandt van Rijn, for example, dedicated a major share of his prodigious output to portraits of Jesus and scenes from his life and ministry. Rembrandt was captivated by the story of the two disciples on the road to Emmaus and their amazing discovery at the end of their journey. "In Rembrandt's haunting images of these subjects," writes art historian George Keyes, "the primary focus is on what the human mind and soul behold."[3]

What they ought to behold, according to Rembrandt and many other admirers, is an individual endowed with sublime wisdom, goodness, and tenderness of heart. Religious leaders, writers, philosophers, scientists, kings, presidents, prime ministers— hardly any educated person has failed to encounter his influence. "Regardless of what anyone may personally think or believe about him," writes historian Jaroslav Pelikan, "Jesus of Nazareth has been the dominant figure in the history of Western culture for almost twenty centuries."[4]

That scholarly judgment, however, would have to wait. Now, as these men retreat from the chaos of events in Jerusalem, the life and mission of Jesus appear to have ended in violent and miserable failure. Suddenly and without warning, he was seized and executed by the Romans, the pagan power occupying Jerusalem and the larger region known as Palestine.[5]

In fact, wherever Jews found themselves in the world, they lived under the heel of Roman rule.[6] Their governors were often brutal, corrupt, and capricious. Like the former Soviet Union, the Roman Empire groomed local administrators from among their conquered people to act as their eyes and ears. Often these hand-picked lackeys ruled as despots, as did King Herod during his thirty-three-year reign. The Jewish historian Josephus described Herod as "cruel to all alike" and "contemptuous of justice."

Even so, it was simply incomprehensible to these disciples that Jesus could be judged and condemned to crucifixion. Many of the famous paintings that depict the scene fail to capture the horror of it. Roman crucifixion in the first century was an especially odious way to die. The victim was flogged, often severely, then impaled on a wooden cross with outstretched arms. Given the culture of violence in ancient Rome, he might be further abused and tormented by his executioners. Writes historian Martin Hengel: "Crucifixion was a punishment in which the caprice and sadism of the executioners were given full rein."[7] The victim was stripped naked and exposed to the elements, then left to fight for breath and life as onlookers jeered or expressed voyeuristic pleasure. It was a fate reserved for criminals, rebels, murderers, and miscreants.

How could this happen to Jesus?

Here was a personality whose acts of compassion crashed through the barriers of wealth, status, sex, and religion. Here was a rabbi whose knowledge of God and his kingdom seemed to emerge from deep within the collective genius and goodness of mankind. Hearing him teach was like being led on a fearsome voyage to a bright city at the far end of the world. To go with him meant great danger, yet to remain meant sadness and eternal regret.

Ancient Rome, with its state-sponsored polytheism, is often noted for its tolerance of other faiths. The Jews, who distinguished themselves by their exclusive belief in God, were exempt from laws demanding that the emperor be worshipped as a deity. Yet Caesar's tolerance had severe limits; anyone who challenged the authority of the emperor—by refusing to pay taxes, for example—was a target for arrest and execution. The Roman principle of occupation was simple: use massive force to put down a revolt before it spread. That's exactly the fate that recently befell a group of about two thousand Jews who were crucified en masse in Galilee, a district with a reputation for rebellion.

The critics of Jesus, in fact, sometimes called him "the Galilean" to mark him as a troublemaker. So it is not hard to imagine why the Romans might have viewed Jesus as a threat. Though his public ministry had begun only a few years earlier, he drew crowds that numbered in the tens of thousands, from Phoenicia in the north to Judea in the south. Normal life seemed to grind to a halt whenever people gathered to hear him preach. His presence in Jerusalem, another hotbed of civic unrest, was electrifying. There were rumors that Jesus and his inner circle were getting ready to lead a rebellion.

Surely anyone who could command such devotion constituted a political problem. Perhaps a confrontation was inevitable. It seems that Jesus did, after all, claim to be a king—the king of the Jews—and the emperor could not abide a rival for long.

All of that was bad enough. What was inconceivable, what shocked these men to the core, was that Israel's religious leaders were collaborators in this spectacle.

The Scribes and the Pharisees represented all that was revered and holy in the Jewish faith. Like most of their fellow Jews, they quietly regarded Roman rule as abhorrent, especially when it collided with their religious customs. They had publicly clashed with the governor, Pontius Pilate, over his recent seizure of money from the temple treasury. Yet these same individuals, Israel's defenders, orchestrated the arrest and trial of Jesus. They even demanded his execution by the Roman authorities. "If you let this man go," they warned the governor, "you are no friend of Caesar."[8]

It was too much to bear. So these friends set out for home, to Emmaus.

Wouldn't many of us do the same? When a great crisis sweeps into our lives, when our dreams turn to powder—wherever we are at that moment—something calls us back home. But is the comfort and security of home all that we seek? We may discover, to our surprise, something else, a desire that is not so easily satisfied. Whether we say it or not, we might soon find ourselves on a quest. "The search is what anyone would undertake if he were not sunk in the everydayness of his own life," writes Walker Percy. "To become aware of the possibility of the search is to be onto something. Not to be onto something is to be in despair."[9]

Sixteen years ago I took a walk down the Emmaus road. It was spring. After suffering a violent seizure, my mother underwent a battery of tests and was diagnosed with cancer. She had a brain tumor, highly malignant—and inoperable. Neither radiation nor chemotherapy was expected to be of much help. But my mother had been a healthy woman all her life, and we hoped that somehow she could overcome it. Instead, for many, many months we watched helplessly as she gradually succumbed to this wretched disease. Italian sons are often very close to their mothers, and I would have gladly—yes, gladly—faced a firing squad if that transaction could have saved my mom's life. But there was nothing to be done.

Not long after Mom died, I made a trip to a little island off the coast of southern Italy. My maternal grandfather, Giuseppe

Aiello, was born on the island of Ventotene, in the Tyrrhenian Sea, about an hour's boat ride from Naples. When he was sixteen years old, he left his home for America and settled in Brooklyn, New York. He opened up a barbershop, married, raised a family, and eventually retired to a small beach house that he built on eastern Long Island. He never looked back.

It was my first visit to Ventotene. Along with me came my father, my mother's sister, Carmella, and her husband Lou. We all had different reasons for wanting to go. I felt a special bond to my grandfather. I was named after him—Giuseppe is Italian for Joseph—and my mother often told me how much she loved her father and missed him after he died. Because I felt the loss of my mother so deeply, and because she was so close to my grandfather, I imagined that at Ventotene I might get a little piece of her back.

As we approached the island, I could almost see Giuseppe dragging his net for minnows, like we used to do when we'd spend a day at the beach together and show off the catch to Mom. As we stepped off the boat, a little Italian boy blurted out what was in my heart: *"Arriviamo! Ventotene! Ventotene!"*

The island seemed to open up its arms to welcome us home. The smell of raw fish, the squawking seagulls, the ragged and rocky cliffs, the uneven steps twisting their way down to a narrow beach—it was much like the little beach town that became the center of my grandfather's life, and my own life as a boy. I realized that Giuseppe Aiello had never forgotten his island home; he carried something of Ventotene with him and gave it to his sons and daughters and their families.

The experience of going home—if it is a good and happy home—not only can be a comfort to us, it also can become a distraction, something that keeps us from fulfilling a great task or obligation set before us. Think of the hobbits in J. R. R. Tolkien's *The Lord of the Rings*, who are faced with the nearly comical prospect of trying to evade the armies of Mordor and take the Ring to the fires of Mount Doom to destroy it. Early in their quest, Frodo and his companions not only must fight off their fear of the dreadful Black Riders, but also endure the forbidding uncertainties of the Old Forest:

> They would soon now be going forward into lands wholly strange to them, and beyond all but the most vague and distant legends of the Shire, and in the gathering twilight they longed for home. A deep loneliness and sense of loss was on them. They stood silent, reluctant to make the final parting.[10]

The lure of returning home almost causes Frodo to evade the great calling on his life, with all the challenges and sorrows it will bring. So, too, perhaps, with the friends on the Emmaus road. They feel that something of the greatest consequence has come into their lives—something to which they'd become deeply devoted—but now it all seems wrong, horribly wrong, and they want to escape from it.

We don't know much about these men. One of them is called Cleopas, who apparently was well-known among the followers of Jesus. The identity of the other man is not given, perhaps because to do so would have meant trouble for him and his family. Yet, as we'll see, we can infer much about them as we learn more of the circumstances of their flight from Jerusalem.[11] We may, in fact, come to recognize much of ourselves in them and in their struggle. "They are real people," writes biblical scholar Michael Wilcock, "and among them the human condition is really to be found."[12]

Their journey likely began in silence. The events of the last forty-eight hours have rendered words useless, almost a violation, like a clumsy intrusion upon a grieving widow. Yet they must speak. Although we're not given all the details of what they say to one another, we have a partial record: an exchange between two followers of Jesus of Nazareth, uttered just days after his execution, about the longings of the human heart and the mysterious purposes of God's heart. For its realism and transparency, this conversation on the road to Emmaus must rank as one of the most remarkable pieces of prose in ancient literature.

An exaggeration? Perhaps. The Greeks and Romans, of course, have given us great mythologies and histories. Thanks to Homer, we're still impressed by "the wily Odysseus," who uses his gift of speech to outwit his foes and make his way home to his beloved Penelope. From Thucydides, an eyewitness to the Peloponnesian War, we learn how an all-encompassing conflict transforms the character of nations, lessons still taught in our military academies. In the meditations of Marcus Aurelius, we find a soldier-emperor confronting the frailty of human life, and all its supposed achievements, with mystic stoicism. "Look at the swiftness of the oblivion of all men; the gulf of endless time, behind and before; the hollowness of applause, the fickleness and folly of those who seem to speak well of you, and the narrow room in which it is confined," he wrote. "This should make you pause."[13]

But here, in this scene recorded in the gospel of Luke, we have a story that contains all these elements and yet seems to transcend them. It is a work of reportage that reveals a probing and contemplative mind, a gift for narrative detail, a poet's heart for meaning and healing and love. And even more: we are led to believe that a great mystery—some unapproachable truth about the human condition—is finally about to be revealed.

The account of these friends on the Emmaus road is, admittedly, sparse. We seem to be told only what we need to know. Yet their discussion, joined by a third man—a stranger—comes to us with singular force. What follows is a layman's reflection on the meaning of that exchange, a story of hope, despondency, and faith. It is a story latent with insight for the believer, as well as the honest skeptic.

Its significance seems especially important for our own day, a period marked not only by religious zealotry, but also by massive indifference to matters of the spirit. Many people seem too content with the quality of their faith, certain that nothing should disturb it. For them, their beliefs require no examination. Others, though, have given up any hope of discovering truths about God that they can hang on to. For them, there are no certainties in the realm of religion; it seems best to muddle through without them. Menachem Mendel, a rabbi in the nineteenth century, put it this way: "For the believer there are no questions, and for the unbeliever there are no answers."[14]

That claim, however, doesn't ring true for most of us. Life has a way of forcing painful questions upon us, whether we welcome them or not. And the human heart has a way of keeping alive in us the longing for answers. To extinguish this hope, either through neglect or cold rationality, would seem to diminish what it means to be human. The road to Emmaus, after all, is a road all of us find ourselves on—eventually. It is the path of every pilgrim who tries to make sense of the wilderness of the world around him.

"As I watched, there awoke in me an immense curiosity," writes Percy. "I was onto something."[15]

1

THINGS SEEN AND UNSEEN

"As they talked and discussed these things
with each other, Jesus himself came up and
walked along with them; but they were kept
from recognizing him."

———⊷◆⊷———

A bizarre scene greets one of Europe's leading Catholic scholars, John Colet, as he approaches the famous cathedral in Canterbury, England. The year is around 1511, a time of anxious spirituality in Catholic Europe.

It was here, nearly 350 years earlier, that an exasperated King Henry II had reached the limits of his royal patience with an obdurate churchman named Thomas Becket. The two had become embroiled in a protracted and testy church-state debate, and Becket refused to yield. "Will no one rid me of that turbulent priest?" complained the king. Four of Henry's knights responded by attacking Becket in his cathedral, stabbing him to death. The Church quickly venerated him as a martyr and a saint. An elaborate gold-studded shrine was built in his honor. Plays, novels, operas, and eventually, Hollywood filmmakers would tell his story of defiance.

Becket's shrine became the most important place of pilgrimage for Catholics in England in the centuries after his death. And so, in a gesture of reverence, Colet decides to pay a visit to the site. As the dean of St. Paul's Cathedral in London, Colet is a pious believer and defender of the Church.

Yet nothing has prepared him for what he sees in Canterbury.

After Becket was murdered, local people managed to acquire pieces of cloth soaked in his blood. Rumors spread that, when touched by this cloth, people were cured of blindness, epilepsy, leprosy, and other ailments. Before long, the monks at Canterbury were selling small glass bottles of Becket's blood to distressed visitors. Geoffrey Chaucer described the scene in The Canterbury Tales:

> *And specially from every shire's end*
> *Of England they to Canterbury went,*
> *The holy blessed martyr there to seek*
> *Who helped them when they lay so ill and weak.[1]*

The Becket blood vendors are in full swing when Colet arrives. Noisy salesmen at souvenir stalls hawk metal trinkets as proof of a spiritual pilgrimage. A beggar sprinkles Colet with holy water and holds out what he claims is Becket's shoe for him to kiss and receive a blessing. Colet is appalled. "Do these fools expect us to kiss the shoe of every good man who ever lived?" he complains. "Why not bring us their spittle or their dung to be kissed?"[2]

What is it that makes people build shrines, collect relics, preserve the blood of martyrs, and travel to faraway places to touch the bones of long-dead individuals thought to be close to God?

Why, for that matter, are there an estimated twenty-five thousand Elvis Presley impersonators gyrating their hips to hysterical crowds around the globe? Busloads of fans trek to his gravesite at Graceland in Memphis, Tennessee, with the enthusiasm of a Canterbury pilgrim. Shrines to the music legend multiply every year. Elvis paraphernalia is gobbled up as greedily as Becket blood samples ever were. There's even a "24-Hour Church of Elvis" in Portland, Oregon (I'm guessing "Love Me Tender" is their number one hymn). Erika Doss, who interviewed scores of fans for her book *Elvis Culture*, wrote that the icon is "imagined as a special, wondrous, virtuous, transcendent and even miraculous figure."[3]

What explains the near deification of this rock 'n' roll legend? Crackpot spirituality? Emotionally stunted individuals? Johnny Carson once quipped: "If life was fair, Elvis would still be alive and all the impersonators would be dead."[4]

Yet to blame this phenomenon on superstitions or psychology doesn't explain very much. Apparently there is something about everyday life—even in our most satisfying moments—that leaves many people anxious for something else. There seems to be a powerful impulse in human nature to connect with a "wondrous, virtuous, transcendent" figure: to be in the presence of God.

The God-Seekers

This is one of the most striking facts for those of us who study the history of civilizations. Every civilization is shaped by what philosopher Huston Smith calls its "God-seekers," those individuals who try to make contact with the divine. Every civilization, without fail, develops an elaborate system of religious beliefs that help to hold human societies together. "What a strange fellowship this is," Smith writes, "the God-seekers in every land, lifting their voices in the most disparate way imaginable to the God of all life."[5]

The Jews in Jesus' day were especially earnest in their quest to know God. They built a massive and ornate temple in Jerusalem, where they employed priests who offered sacrifices to purify their hearts before Jehovah. Their sacred text, the Torah, records dramatic encounters between God and his people. Although God is never visualized by the Jews—never represented in art in any form—he is nonetheless described, tenaciously, as a Person. King, Redeemer, Defender, Judge, Father, Shepherd—all these images are applied to him.

The entire history of Judaism can be read as a long, tortuous tale of a nation's attempt to know God and to be blessed by him. Does this explain what is happening on the road to Emmaus? *"Jesus himself came up and walked along with them; but they were kept from recognizing him."* We are informed, without any grandiosity and with no explanation, that Jesus has somehow returned to life and appeared among these disciples.

Were these fervent believers being carried away by their desire for an encounter with the supernatural? They wouldn't be the first. We marvel at the architectural achievements of the ancient Egyptians, for example, whose massive stone pyramids still baffle modern engineers. The Great Pyramid at Giza reaches 480 feet into the sky—taller than a forty-story skyscraper—and is composed of over two million blocks of limestone. Think of it: thousands of workers hauled tens of thousands of tons of stone across vast stretches of desert over many decades to build these wonders.

And for what purpose? A hieroglyphic text, addressed to the Egyptian god Atum, explains the reason: "O Atum, put your arms around King Neferkare Pepy II, around this construction work, around this pyramid . . . . May you guard lest anything happen to him evilly [sic] throughout the course of eternity."[6] In other words, the pyramids served as burial chambers to help Egyptian kings make a successful journey from death to the afterlife. In this case, King Pepy II wanted to arrive safely in paradise—and mobilized an army of slaves and civil engineers to make it happen.

Likewise, we admire the political and military accomplishments of ancient Rome—its republican ideals, territorial conquests, and the "Pax Romana" that brought stability to much of the known world. We know the Romans had a panoply of "gods" and "goddesses," many of them borrowed from the Greeks. But their deities seem so much like human projections—they could be as devious and corruptible as a Nero or a Caligula—that we suspect no one really took them seriously.

Here it's worth remembering that the most important myth for the Romans was Virgil's *The Aeneid*, an epic poem about sacrifice, suffering, loyalty, and obedience to the gods. The hero of the story, Aeneas is described as "a man outstanding in his piety." Aeneas achieves true greatness, in fact, only when he submits fully to the will of the gods and devotes himself with absolute purity to his mission, the establishment of a new political society in Rome. Thus, when Aeneas allows his lover Dido to distract him from his task, it requires a stern visitation from the gods to get him back on course. "But Aeneas is driven by duty now," Virgil writes. "Strongly as he longs to ease and allay her sorrow, speak to her, turn away her anguish with reassurance, still, moaning deeply, heart shattered by his great love, in spite of all he obeys the gods' commands and back he goes to his ships."[7]

This is what the Romans meant by piety. The story of Aeneas—a man mindful of the gods as he pursues his calling—was adopted throughout the empire as the pattern of the Roman hero.

The Faith of Fox Mulder

The fact is that every society, in its own way, reaches out for God.

The Jews in Jesus' day were very much like, but also very different from, the other cultures around them. Virtually every other society viewed nature as divine. The list of gods and goddesses, representing every aspect of the physical world, was endless. No matter where we look—among the Babylonians, Egyptians, Persians, Greeks, or Romans—we find people worshipping nature as the living and breathing embodiment of divinity.

Not the Jews. The opening pages of Genesis assert the non-divinity of the cosmos: "In the beginning, God . . ." The heavens and the earth are not eternal. They came into existence, we are told, from the hand of a Being outside of them, a Creator utterly distinct from his creation. While other religions assumed the presence of deities all about them, the religion of the Jews began in a radically different place. Jewish philosopher Leon Kass says the opening lines of Scripture set Judaism at odds with the rest of the known world: "This perfectly natural human tendency the Bible seeks to oppose, and right from the first verse, by denying that the heavens—or any other beings—are worthy of human reverence."[8]

In another sense, though, the Jews are like people in other societies. They, too, are God-seekers. More importantly, they believed firmly that they had discovered the one true God—that they were known and favored by him among all the peoples of the earth. They championed the idea that God is not only personal but purposeful, a Supreme Being with a supremely moral agenda for mankind. Scholar Paul Johnson calls the introduction of this idea "one of the great turning points in history, perhaps the greatest of all."[9]

Thus, at first glance, the encounter on the road to Emmaus is baffling. We assume that people living in the first century AD were more prone to spiritual "experiences" than we are as enlightened, sensible, modern people. The Jews accepted the possibility of such experiences. Surely these followers of Jesus, we reason, are desperate for some sign of hope after his brutal execution, some message from heaven to reassure them that their faith in him was not a tragic fantasy. They want to believe.

Many scholars of the Bible treat the accounts of Jesus' death and resurrection in just this way: the disconsolate disciples will believe almost anything in order to regain their psychological equilibrium. Their frame of mind, we are told, is like that of Fox

Mulder, the credulous FBI agent from the TV show *The X-Files*. A recurring theme of the series was a haunting memory from Mulder's childhood, when his sister was mysteriously abducted by aliens from outer space. Mulder's faith in the existence of UFOs was constantly reinforced by his desire to find his sister alive. A poster over his desk with a picture of a UFO carried this caption: "I want to believe."

But if this was the psychological mood of these two men on the Emmaus road, then we're faced with a very odd tale indeed. *"Jesus himself came up and walked along with them; but they were kept from recognizing him."* What can this mean? If these disciples are so anxious for a spiritual experience—a supernatural reunion with Jesus, for example—then why aren't they immediately overwhelmed with fear, shock, or joy at seeing Jesus alive?

We'll explore later the likelihood of ordinary Jews, even followers of Jesus, believing in a resurrected Messiah. For now, let's admit that although we're a long way from the people who lived in the first century, we share at least one thing in common. We often have a hard time recognizing the spiritual dimension to life. Whatever else they believed about the supernatural, these disciples had to face a world of physical hardships that often left little room for thoughts of God. Indeed, many Jews in Jesus' day complained that the God of Abraham had abandoned his people. As one of their prophets lamented: "You have covered yourself with a cloud so that no prayer can get through."[10]

The two men in our story must have asked the same question we ask: If God exists, if there is no place in the universe where he is not present, then why does he seem so absent from our everyday experience?

The Scientific Spirit

The question is a painful one for many of us. Perhaps it is made more painful in a society that owes so much to the scientific quest: a search for knowledge that, by definition, must exclude any thoughts of the supernatural. The tools of modern science—reason, observation, experimentation—have brought countless blessings into our lives. Who would want to step into a dentist's chair, without anesthesia, and have his wisdom teeth extracted? Nevertheless, the assumptions of science have changed dramatically over the centuries, in ways that can close off our minds to the wonder and mystery of life.

It is important to remember that the earliest scientists, those pioneering thinkers of the later Middle Ages, saw themselves as religious believers in pursuit of the secrets of creation. Virtually all of the early innovators of the period—Kepler, Copernicus, Galileo, and Newton—believed that God sought to reveal himself through man's exploration of the physical universe.

"They perceived their intellectual breakthroughs as foundational contributions to a sacred mission," writes philosopher Richard Tarnas. "Their scientific discoveries were triumphant spiritual awakenings to the divine architecture of the world, revelations of the true cosmic order."[11] Newton, whose law of universal gravitation laid the foundation for modern science, argued that the "the frame of nature" strongly suggested a universe designed and sustained by God. For Newton, nature reinforced the existence of a Deity who should be worshipped for "the creating, preserving, and governing of all things according to his good will and pleasure."[12]

Some Christian thinkers, though, began to claim too much from nature. They argued that all living things bore the mark of divine benevolence. They insisted that the natural world, in all its details, proved the existence of a loving Creator. Others, however, looked at the same universe and saw the virtual absence of God—a world that ran on its own steam, often with appalling ruthlessness.

The discoveries in biology by Charles Darwin in the nineteenth century seemed to confirm the growing skepticism. The relentless struggle for survival through evolution—whereby the strongest and ablest organisms devoured the weakest—ran afoul of the God of Mercy. Had Darwin written a Beatitude, it might have been this: "Blessed are the cunning, the brutal, and the heartless, for they shall inherit the earth."

Over time, religious belief became more and more removed from the scientific quest. Even if God existed, the new scientists reasoned, he was indifferent to the world he had made. Neither the laws of nature nor the principles of science required the assistance of a Creator. "The more we know of the fixed laws of nature," wrote Darwin, "the more incredible do miracles become."[13] It would not be long before nearly the entire scientific community would agree with him. As philosopher Peter Gay has written, science seemed to have all the facts on its side—and none of those facts involved a deity. "Science could give the deists and the atheists great comfort and supply them with what they wanted—Newton's physics without Newton's God."[14]

Not all modern scientists, of course, have looked at the universe, with all its complexity, and deduced God's absence. When pressed, Albert Einstein denied he was an atheist, explaining that he preferred an attitude of humility toward the cosmos, given "the weakness of our intellectual understanding" of ourselves and the natural world around us:

> We are in the position of a little child entering a huge library filled with books in many languages. The child knows someone must have written those books. It does not know how . . . The child dimly suspects a mysterious order in the arrangement of the books but doesn't know what it is. That, it seems to me, is the attitude of even the most intelligent human being toward God. We see the universe marvelously arranged and obeying certain laws but only dimly understand these laws.[15]

More recently, a new generation of scientists has identified an "anthropic principle" at work in the universe, the arrangement of physical laws that seem uncannily suited to support human life. Advanced by physicists such as John Barrow and Frank Tipler, they discern "a life-giving factor" at the center of the machinery of the world. "It is not only man that is adapted to the universe," they write. "The universe is adapted to man."[16] Astronomer Sir Fred Hoyle famously admitted that his atheism was shaken by his discovery that carbon atoms seemed fine-tuned to accommodate human life. "A commonsense interpretation of the facts suggests that a superintellect has monkeyed with physics, as well as with chemistry and biology," he concludes, "and that there are no blind forces worth speaking about in nature."[17]

Although such thinkers might hint of an Intelligence behind the universe, this admission doesn't touch the underlying outlook of the modern scientist. By this I mean *scientism*, the belief that science can explain every facet of human existence from nature itself. Under this view, there is simply no role for any Force or Power or Intelligence outside of nature.

This is not the place to debate the merits of scientism. What's important for us is that this mind-set is not confined to men and women in white lab coats. It shapes the unconscious assumptions of nearly everyone living in the West. The spirit of scientism makes the encounter on the road to Emmaus sound like a children's fairy tale, no matter how much it reads to the contrary.

Think about it this way. Natural laws work exceedingly well: They keep airplanes flying and cell phones buzzing. They help tomatoes grow in our gardens and babies grow in their mothers' womb. They seem to explain nearly every phenomenon that appears on the horizon. It is science that has allowed us to understand and harness the natural world, a world that apparently functions without any help from any other world. Although there's an audience for paranormal sleuths on TV shows like *Ghosthunters*, most of us are not inclined to see the supernatural thumping its way through our living rooms. Romantics might credit God with a glorious sunrise; rational people look to the laws of planetary motion.

It is not that the agnostic has a scientific explanation for the big questions about human existence—the origin of life, the tug of conscience, the capacity for love, the fear of death. Evolution, in fact, offers no answers to these questions.

What Darwin and the scientific community offer is an impression, the belief that science can provide answers to all these questions, *eventually*. Richard Dawkins, the celebrated atheist-scientist, in his own account of Darwin's theory, begins his book with more than a touch of hubris in this regard: "This book is written in the conviction that our own existence once presented the greatest of all mysteries, but that it is a mystery no longer because it is solved."[18]

The mystery of human existence has been solved, the scientist declares, and it does not involve anything out of the ordinary, much less the supernatural.

The Hidden God

For most of us, of course, the mystery of human life has not been solved to our satisfaction. The presence of this stranger on the road to Emmaus may be hard to swallow at face value. But the possibility of "God in disguise"—the supernatural mingling with the natural—is also hard to ignore.

Beginning at least from the 1920s, Hollywood writers and filmmakers have found the topic of the presence of God irresistible. Mary Lea Bandy, curator of the film department at the Museum of Modern Art, and Antonio Monda, film professor at New York University, began asking themselves a question: Is God, his presence or absence, the inner core of any story?

They soon identified numerous films—by directors ranging from Alfred Hitchcock to Roberto Rossellini—with spiritual themes. "Film history tells us that a hidden God can take the form of a donkey bearing all human misery on its shoulders," they write, "or of a starship that, after many close encounters, finally reaches us and changes our lives."[19] The two organized a film exhibit called "The Hidden God: Film and Faith," which drew thousands of visitors to the Museum of Modern Art during its three-month run.

One of the films featured in the exhibit was *Babette's Feast* (1987), based on a short story by Isak Dinesen. It tells of an experience involving Babette Hersant, a terrified woman who flees the violence of the Paris Commune in 1871 to a village in the far north of Denmark. There Babette encounters a cast of characters hardened by hypocrisy, self-absorption, and loveless religion. She is taken into the home of two woeful sisters, Martine and Filippa, daughters of the founder of an austere religious brotherhood.

To celebrate the founder's one hundredth anniversary, Babette—a master chef—offers to cook an extravagant French dinner. Using her winnings from a lottery, she has a litany of goods shipped in by boat: ice, dishes, glasses, linen, cheeses and meats, cases of wine, and a very large turtle—destined for the soup bowl.

The dinner scene evokes the splendor of a wedding banquet, an image that occurs often in the Bible to describe God's fellowship with his people, brought safely and finally home. The richness and joy of the meal transforms the guests from gloomy and petty souls into people who have tasted divine mercy. "The moment comes when our eyes are opened, and we see and realize that grace is infinite," says General Löwenhielm. "Grace, my friends, demands nothing from us but that we shall await it with confidence and acknowledge it in gratitude . . . grace takes us all to its bosom and proclaims general amnesty."

The hidden God reveals himself, even partially, in a meal prepared with love and sacrifice.

Christian thinkers were exploring this theme—the mysterious presence or absence of God—long before Hollywood got into the act. The mystics of the Middle Ages referred to God as "a cloud of unknowing," a Being ultimately mysterious and never fully approachable.[20] Protestant reformer Martin Luther, writing in the 1520s, also described "the hidden God" of the Bible, a God so awesome that he cannot directly reveal himself to human beings without overwhelming us. For this reason, Luther wrote, God keeps himself partially hidden, even to those who seek him.

There is a strong dose of humility among the best of these authors, a willingness to admit the limits of our ability to understand God and how he might interact with our world. "I recommend that speculations be laid aside," wrote Luther, "and I should like to have this rule adhered to after my death."[21]

Here we must acknowledge, with sadness, that the Christian church has produced many pastors and theologians who have ignored Luther's rule. They assure us, with cold logic and hot sermons, that they know perfectly well why many people feel so alienated from God. The reality, we are told, is that God has rejected those people. *He has hidden himself so that he cannot be found by them.* God will reveal himself to a chosen few but has destined the rest of the human race to eternal darkness and futility.

Whatever the good intentions of these individuals, something has gone wrong with their entire approach to the God of the Bible. They have confused their own prejudices and speculations with the teachings of Jesus. Let's not mince words. The notion that God would conceal himself so that people could never find him, that he would take pleasure in abandoning human souls to utter desolation—here is an idea that seems to have bubbled up from the lava pit of hell itself.

The faith according to Jesus offers a very different account of God's heart.

What was it, after all, that attracted our two friends to Jesus in the first place? It was not his promise to weed out the sinful from the righteous. It was not his threat to punish with hellfire all those who resisted his message. There was something else that drew them, something like a brave song from childhood, half-forgotten but still able to fill the heart with courage. "I am a Jew," confessed Einstein, "but I am enthralled by the luminous figure of the Nazarene."[22]

What drew these men to Jesus? The Jewish faith, the Scripture that helped shape the mind of the Nazarene, describes God's determination to seek out lost people, to reveal himself to them, and to bring them to safety. Shockingly stern warnings appear in the Torah about the fate of God's enemies—there awaits a dreadful judgment for those who are too proud to see their need for him. But in the Old Testament we also find some of the most tenderhearted images of God in the entire Bible:

> I myself will search for my sheep and look after them. As a shep-
> herd looks after his scattered flock when he is with them, so will I
> look after my sheep. I will rescue them from all the places where
> they were scattered on a day of clouds and darkness. . . . I will
> search for the lost and bring back the strays. I will bind up the
> injured and strengthen the weak.[23]

When Jesus the Jew wanted to explain God's attitude toward lost people—those who felt abandoned by him—he borrowed the same image from the Hebrew Bible. "I am the good shepherd," he told them. "The good shepherd lays down his life for the sheep."[24] His emphasis was on the shepherd's quest to reclaim those who had lost their way. "The revolution promised in the

Old Testament is one in which God intervenes to rescue his lost sheep," writes Oxford theologian David Wenham. "Jesus claims to have brought that revolution."[25]

On one occasion Jesus was approached by religious leaders who complained about the people he had chosen as his friends—unsavory "sinners" who couldn't possibly be accepted by God. But Jesus had bad news for the religious establishment: they didn't understand divine mercy.

The Teacher told them three stories in succession to shatter their misconceptions. The first was about a shepherd who lost one of his sheep and left behind the rest to recover him. The second story was about a woman who lost a precious silver coin and tore her house upside down to find it. The last story described a father who lost his son to a life of reckless living— the prodigal son—but who threw a banquet to celebrate his homecoming. Each tale ends the same way, with joy over what has been reclaimed and redeemed. "In the same way, I tell you," Jesus said, "there is rejoicing in the presence of the angels of God over one sinner who repents."[26]

It is a theme of rescue that speaks to us still.

In the 2008 movie *Taken*, Liam Neeson plays Bryan Mills, a retired CIA officer whose daughter, Kim, is kidnapped while on vacation in Paris. He tells her captors he will use every skill, every scrap of knowledge, every resource at his disposal to find her and bring her home. He warns them he will hunt them down and kill them if anything happens to his daughter.

The man is true to his word. Bryan becomes a sleepless force of nature, a father who is single-minded in his devotion to one thing: to get his daughter back. After dispatching numerous thugs and degenerates, almost dead from injury and exhaustion himself, he finds his daughter alive, on board a yacht, sold as a prostitute to an Arab sheik. "Daddy, you came for me," she says, collapsing into his arms. Almost overcome with joy and relief, he says simply: "I told you I would."

In a much older film, *The Searchers* (1956), a John Ford Western, we witness a man's relentless quest to recover a young girl kidnapped by Indians. John Wayne plays Ethan Edwards, an ex-Confederate soldier who returns home to start his life over. But when his niece, Debbie (Natalie Wood), is abducted by Commanches, he immediately sets off on a rescue mission. Set in Texas in the 1860s, Ethan's search carries him through barren and thirsty landscapes, across hundreds of miles, from one desperate year to the next. It will claim the lives of his companions and nearly rob him of his own.

Film critic Edward Buscombe calls *The Searchers* "one of the great masterpieces of American cinema."[27] *New York* magazine ranks it as the most influential movie in American history.[28] What explains the film's remarkable appeal?

Ethan is a man nearly consumed with hatred for the Indians. When he discovers his brother's ranch burned to the ground— the family ravaged and murdered by Commanches—we see an individual burdened not only by grief, but also by a dark brooding that never leaves him. He knows that Debbie, if she is alive, will take on the ways of the Indians. The thought fills him with anger and loathing. "Livin' with Commanches ain't being alive," he says.

And yet Ethan keeps up his pursuit with a resolve that yields to nothing and no one. "We'll find them in the end, I promise you," he tells his nephew, "just as sure as the turning of the earth." It is an epic search, and we're never certain until the end whether Ethan intends to rescue his niece or to put a bullet in her head.

When Ethan finally finds his niece, alive in an Indian camp, he seems gripped by a force he cannot control. Terrified by what he might do, Debbie tries to flee. He corners her, seizes her small, slender body in his broad hands, and lifts her up to the sky. Is there room for love in his heart—or only hate? It is a fearsome, breathless moment. And then, in an instant, Ethan drops the girl down into his arms and says, "Let's go home, Debbie."

The Mystery That Remains

The God of Jesus, as we are led to believe from the Bible, is something like this—fearsome and yet forgiving, a God who does not rest until he recovers those who have lost their way. What first brought these men on the Emmaus road into the company of Jesus? It was love that drew them. This seems to be the starting place for clear thinking about God's dealings with us in the world. "In Jesus, God has taken the initiative to seek out the sinner, to bring the lost into the blessing of his reign," writes biblical scholar George Eldon Ladd. In the faith according to Jesus, "God is the seeking God."[29]

Yet we are still left with a mystery about his presence in our lives, aren't we?

The story of these disciples suggests something of it. *"Jesus himself came up and walked along with them; but they were kept from recognizing him."* Here, in the middle of a conversation, a stranger appears. We are told the stranger is Jesus, alive from the dead and yet unrecognized by his friends. Why might God work in this way? Why doesn't he just announce himself and get on with his agenda?

Perhaps we can learn something about the character of God from this encounter, something about his methods with ordinary people like us. He will not coerce us. He does not normally overwhelm our senses. Even a thinker such as Blaise Pascal, an intensely religious man living in an intensely religious age, was often staggered by the vast emptiness of the universe: "I am terrified by the eternal silence of these infinite spaces."[30]

The Bible contains stories of startling visitations from God—we think of Moses and the burning bush or the apostle Paul on the road to Damascus. But there are not many stories like this in Scripture, and the vast majority of mortals described in its pages never hear directly from the Almighty. Maybe we've heard a pastor promise us that we will "see the hand of God" in our lives as soon as we decide we want to. What strikes me about some of these preachers is that they probably couldn't recognize the hand of God if it popped them on the nose. They're just too in love with their own ideas about how he works.

There are some among us, of course, who cannot abide the idea of a Creator who continually involves himself in his creation. To them, such a Being would denigrate human initiative and creativity. "In a creative universe God would betray no trace of his presence, since to do so would be to rob [individuals] of their independence, to turn them from the active pursuit of answers to mere supplication of God," writes science author Timothy Ferris in *The Whole Shebang*. "And so it is: God's language is silence."[31]

Many of the greatest souls in history—philosophers and reformers, theologians and scientists—believed just the opposite. They held firmly to a God who speaks through his creation, who draws near to his people, even if his voice and his presence are often hard to discern. Israel's King David wrote freely about his sense of abandonment by God—and just as freely about his nearness.

> Where can I go from your Spirit?
> Where can I flee from your presence?
> If I go up to the heavens, you are there;
> if I make my bed in the depths, you are there.
> If I rise on the wings of the dawn,
> if I settle on the far side of the sea,
> even there your hand will guide me,
> your right hand will hold me fast.[32]

The story of these men on the Emmaus road encourages a little humility. We are asked to keep our minds open to the possibility of God's nearness. Even more, we are invited to set our hearts on a quest to find him.

Again and again in the Bible is a message about God's dramatic appeal for people everywhere to search for him. From the words of Moses: "But if from there you seek the LORD your God, you will find him if you seek him with all your heart and with all your soul."[33] From the prophet Jeremiah: "You will seek me and find me when you seek me with all your heart."[34] From Ezekiel: "If my people . . . will humble themselves and pray and seek my face and turn from their wicked ways, then I will hear from heaven, and I will forgive their sin."[35] From

King David: "For you, LORD, have never forsaken those who seek you."[36]

These two companions are deeply troubled and confused about God, but they have not abandoned their desire to know him. Here the Divine Life steps softly into the flow of ordinary human life. *"As they talked . . . Jesus himself came up and walked along with them."* Maybe this is how most of us, if we were inclined, would have to be introduced to the supernatural. We'd have to begin with the natural.

Thus we read of two friends, on a journey, caught up in a conversation that takes a very sharp turn. These men are not engaged in some "spiritual" exercise. They are not praying. They are not on their way to a monastic retreat. They may be talking about theology, but it's just as likely they are debating politics. Whatever else is going on in their minds, they're not ready for God to show up.

"The perception of the glory is a rare occurrence in our lives. We fail to wonder, we fail to respond to the presence," writes Jewish theologian Abraham Joshua Heschel. "Life is routine, and routine is resistance to the wonder."[37]

Whatever resistance these men have to the wonder of the supernatural, it is about to be challenged—but not directly, not with a flash of light or a voice from heaven. For reasons we can only partly grasp, God does not operate this way with most of us. Perhaps Pascal got closest to the truth of the thing, closer than either the scientific skeptics or the religious dogmatists: "What can be seen on earth indicates neither the total absence, nor the manifest presence of divinity, but the presence of a hidden God," he wrote. "Everything bears this stamp."[38]

2

A Grief Observed

"He asked them, 'What are you discussing
together as you walk along?' They stood still,
their faces downcast."

⟶•◆•⟵

*It is the spring of 1756. An African named Olaudah Equiano, an eleven-
year-old boy who has never left his village, is kidnapped by slave traders.
The plan is to transport him, along with hundreds of other native Africans, across the Atlantic Ocean to the West Indies, where he will work in
the sugarcane fields, or to one of the American colonies to harvest cotton
or tobacco. Either way, he will spend the rest of his life as a slave.*

*Equiano has the great misfortune of living in what is now Nigeria,
the vortex of the infamous Slave Trade Triangle of the eighteenth century. In Great Britain alone, hundreds of ships, thousands of sailors,
and hundreds of millions of pounds of sterling are caught up annually
in the noxious business of human trafficking. At its peak, the slave trade
claims the lives of roughly sixty thousand Africans every year—men,
women, and children who succumb to disease or brutalities during the
ocean voyage. "So much misery condensed in so little room," observed*

abolitionist William Wilberforce, "is more than the human imagination has ever before conceived."[1]

Snatched along with Equiano is his sister, the companion of his youth, whom he loves deeply. They are sold to different slave traders. Equiano probably leaves from Barbados on the sloop Nancy, arriving in Virginia; the fate of his sister is not known. Eventually—remarkably—he gains his freedom and writes about his experiences in a book that becomes an international bestseller. The moment when Equiano and his sister are separated—never to see each other again—comprises a tale of human suffering that shocks the conscience of Christian Europe and strengthens the cause of abolition.

Here, in plain and honest prose, is a grief observed:

> It was in vain that we besought them not to part us; she was torn from me, and immediately carried away, while I was left in a state of distraction not to be described. I cried and grieved continually; and for several days did not eat anything but what they forced into my mouth . . . Yes, thou dear partner of all my childish sports! Thou sharer of my joys and sorrows! Happy should I have ever esteemed myself to encounter every misery for you and to procure your freedom by the sacrifice of my own. Though you were early forced from my arms, your image has been always riveted in my heart, from which neither time nor fortune have been able to remove it.[2]

Of all the experiences common to the human condition, it is the experience of grief that denies us the luxury of being spectators, aloof and uncommitted. Romantic love, intense hatred, paralyzing fear—many of us might navigate through many years of our lives without these experiences or, at least, without knowing them in any enduring sense. Grief is different.

Here there is no possibility of evasion. Grief comes into every human life because grief is intimately connected to the brokenness of the world around us. Put another way, sorrow follows naturally from the existence of evil, and no one on earth escapes its long shadow. "Thus have the gods spun the thread for wretched mortals," wrote Homer, "that they live in grief while they themselves are without cares."[3]

No Room for Magical Thinking

Grief is another of those raw facts about the human experience that the Bible treats with unique seriousness, sympathy, and realism. *"They stood still, their faces downcast."* The two friends on the road to Emmaus are men in mourning. They are struggling to comprehend an event that has rent their hearts like broken glass through flesh and bone. It is an impenetrable truth, the death of the Teacher from Nazareth.

Unlike the people described in the Bible, we don't make much time for grief in Western society. We dispatch small armies of "grief counselors" to schools or businesses devastated by tragedy, but to what end? We give sorrow a timeline. We provide mourners with medications. We have stages and strategies for grief. And yet we do everything possible to distract ourselves from the sadness that has invaded our orderly lives.

In *The Year of Magical Thinking*, author Joan Didion tries to make sense of her world after the death of her husband, John

Gregory Dunne. Didion marvels at the capacity of grief "to derange the mind," that is, to throw its victims into a mode of irrationality. They cannot think and live as though the person they loved is really dead. Surely there has been some mistake of diagnosis or identity. "I was thinking as small children think," she writes, "as if my thoughts or wishes had the power to reverse the narrative, change the outcome."[4]

One day Didion was clearing the shelves of her husband's clothes, putting them in stacks to give away to thrift shops. But she couldn't bring herself to give away his shoes. "I stood there for a moment, then realized why: he would need shoes if he was to return."[5]

Whatever the mental state of the two disciples on the Emmaus road, they are in no mood for magical thinking. The graphic death of Jesus in Jerusalem has left no room for it.

One of the most striking elements in the biblical story describes how a Roman guard jabs a spear into the chest of his victim, apparently to be sure he is dead—another example of the empire's lethal efficiency. In John's gospel we read that "blood and water" flowed from the wound.[6] We would expect an account of blood, but why is water mentioned? As any first-year medical student could explain, Jesus probably went into shock after being severely beaten by his captors. His heartbeat would accelerate, causing fluid to gather in the membrane that surrounds the heart, a condition called pericardial effusion. A spear thrust in the upper chest, near the heart, would puncture the membrane, releasing the watery contents.

Here is crude, unemotional reporting, a detail of no theological importance: a quiet fact about how men die when subjected to Rome's methods of execution, recorded for no other reason except someone saw it and remembered it and wrote it down.

Although some have speculated that Jesus did not really die on the cross, the account of the disciples on the Emmaus road leaves no doubt about their views of the matter. Jesus of Nazareth is dead, executed in plain sight. His lifeless body was taken away and laid in a tomb. All these men are left with is their grief, a burden that seems impossible to bear. There is no room for magical thinking. *"They stood still, their faces downcast."*

A Maze of Human Suffering

Who is not touched by the heartbreaks and tragedies of life, be they large or small?

Even children know what it means to mourn, when a favorite pet dies or a best friend moves away. A parent struggles with Alzheimer's, a little girl suffers with leukemia, a head injury sends a teenager into a coma, a car slips out of park and slides down a driveway, killing a toddler—there is no shortage of tragic events in our lives.

Several years ago I remember reading of a "freak accident" that claimed the lives of a pastor and his family. He was driving his Lincoln Town Car down a two-lane country road in Cumberland, Indiana, on New Year's Eve. His wife was next to him, and their three children were in the back. Suddenly, out of nowhere, a tree fell directly on the vehicle, killing everyone inside except the youngest child. "There was no wind that night, no rain or snow, nothing to hasten the fall of the long-dead oak tree that crashed down squarely on the roof of the Lincoln," according to a newspaper report. "They probably never even saw it."[7]

What congregation, if it were honest, would not be shaken by such tragedy?

On March 11, 2011, the world learned of a catastrophic tsunami along the Japanese coast, created by an 8.9 magnitude earthquake. "There was an unusual silence, as though the world had stopped," said Mark Avancena, a survivor. "And then the earthquake started."[8] Thousands perished in the deluge; millions were left homeless or without electricity. Fears of a meltdown of nuclear power plants damaged by the tsunami gripped residents for weeks afterward. Scenes of survivors, distraught at the loss of loved ones, homes, and possessions, flashed around the globe. As a CNN reporter summarized the moment: "Japan is a nation united in its grief."[9]

As I write, a severe famine is ravaging the lives of hundreds of thousands of Somalis while international aid agencies struggle to provide food, water, and medical supplies. In the last three months alone, drought and famine have claimed more than twenty-nine thousand children under the age of five. Countless families living in the hard-hit south, such as that of Kaltum Mohamed, have tried to get their children to the capital, Mogadishu, in time to receive emergency aid. Four of Kaltum's five children died in the attempt. "She crouched next to one of their graves and softly patted and smoothed the mound of earth covering it," according to one account. "She wept, then wiped away her tears. She still has a daughter to try to feed."[10]

It is not only the natural world, of course, that turns against us; our fellow human beings have a tendency to turn against us as well. As Equiano's lament suggests, no institution was more wicked than the international slave trade, designed and administered by men—educated, enlightened, churchgoing Europeans. The evil of chattel slavery produced an ocean of human grief.

Our contemporary evils create their own unique miseries. In the suburbs of Washington, D.C., not far from my home, we learn of the stabbing death of Jane McQuain and a frantic search for her missing son, eleven-year-old William. Each night on television we see the picture of a happy, bright-eyed young boy with his mother. And then the news arrives, and all hope dies: the body of William is found in a field, beaten to death with a baseball bat. McQuain's estranged husband is charged with both murders, a gruesome act that stuns an entire community.

During a summer of protests over the 2009 Iranian elections, student demonstrators confront government security forces in Tehran. A twenty-six-year-old musician, Neda Agha-Soltan, is shot in the chest by the Iranian Revolutionary Guard. A doctor rushes to her side, but Neda bleeds to death in less than two minutes, a scene of grief and horror captured on camera and witnessed by millions on the Internet. The killing of "the voice of Iran" becomes one of the most widely witnessed deaths in history, and it turns millions of Iranians into mourners.[11]

In a world hardwired for instant communication, painful and tragic experiences such as these—wherever they occur—ultimately intrude into our lives. Each of them reminds us of the stunning universality of grief—how it looks the same in every society, every language, and every religion in the world.

Where are we to search for wisdom in this maze of human suffering?

Many people turn to faith—and eventually turn away. One can hardly blame them. Religious authorities often seem to be of two minds about the reality of suffering. They are either completely dumbfounded or supremely confident about its meaning. Instead of offering guidance, or even empathy, they dish out pious platitudes, theological abstractions, or icy warnings about God's judgment.

Who can forget the outpouring of grief in the hours and days after the 9/11 terrorist attacks on New York and Washington, D.C.? Yet in that moment of national mourning, two Christian ministers from the political right, Jerry Falwell and Pat Robertson, proclaimed the judgment of God upon an immoral United States: "God continues to lift the curtain and allow the enemies of America to give us probably what we deserve." On the political left, theologian Stanley Hauerwas also saw divine retribution—a punishment for U.S. foreign policy: "The price that Americans are going to have to pay for the kind of arrogance that we are operating out of right now is going to be terrible indeed . . . and I think we will well deserve it."[12]

Thus, even as the pulverized remains of the victims were being recovered from Ground Zero, self-appointed prophets issued God's verdict on the nation. For many Americans, no doubt, it seemed a perversion of faith: to seize upon a moment of human tragedy for the sake of a religious-political agenda.

The problem, of course, is not politics. The problem is presumption. Rather than walking in grief with their neighbors, religious leaders often stand above it all, certain they know the ultimate purpose of suffering.

One Sunday at a church I attended on Capitol Hill, the senior pastor turned the task of delivering the sermon over to a twenty-five-year-old protégé, a seminary graduate with an advanced degree in Cranky Calvinism. The sermon was on the problem of suffering, taken from the Old Testament book of Job. From what any of us could tell, the most painful experience this earnest man had ever known in his young life was the trauma of teenage acne. Yet his message on the mystery of suffering was confident, theologically precise, intellectually rigorous—and utterly detached from the everyday struggles of the people before him.

Even if religious leaders are not certain about the meaning of sorrow in our lives, they often talk as if they are. They hope to make us true believers like themselves. It is as if they are afraid that deep grief will lead only to intractable doubt.

Wiser men have known better. After his wife, Joy, died of cancer, Christian author C. S. Lewis kept a journal, a raw record of his unruly emotions and his great struggle with questions of faith. "I not only live each endless day in grief," he writes, "but live each day thinking about living each day in grief." Lewis described grief as something like the sensation of being afraid: the same queasiness in the stomach, the same unsettledness. "And grief still feels like fear. Perhaps, more strictly, like suspense. Or like waiting; just hanging about waiting for something to happen. It gives life a permanently provisional feeling. It doesn't seem worth starting anything."[13]

Early in the book we read of Lewis's sense of abandonment by God, as if he were knocking on a door that was locked and bolted from the inside. The longer he waited for an answer, the more emphatic the silence became. Lewis explains that his great fear was not that he will cease believing in God, but rather that he will come to believe things about him that aren't true.[14]

All of us who have known great loss understand exactly what he means. The daily sorrow of watching my mom struggle with the pain of cancer, the growing fear of losing the struggle, the sense of helplessness—it all bore down on me like a storm. Grief assaults us, allows us no rest, not even in our dreams. When we grieve, even breathing seems like hard labor. My mom's cancer did not turn me into an agnostic. I continued to believe that God existed; I prayed to him daily. But the suspicion that God simply wasn't who I imagined he was—not nearly so intimate and compassionate as I believed—was terribly hard to shake off.

The Indifferent Universe

It is easy to imagine the companions on the Emmaus road, men of faith, contending with the same doubts and emotions. *"He asked them, 'What are you discussing together as you walk along?' They stood still, their faces downcast."*

When the stranger appears and asks them what they have been talking about on their journey, they not only reveal their sorrow but are taken aback. A catastrophe has befallen Israel. A prophet—or, at least, a man who seemed to be a prophet—has died a shameful death at the hands of pagans. His mission, the dream of Israel restored, has died along with him. Through it all, God has remained absent from the scene.

But the stranger appears unaware of all this, and the disciples are almost offended by his ignorance. *"Are you only a visitor to Jerusalem and do not know the things that have happened there in these days?"* In other words, it would have been impossible for anyone who had been in the Holy City over the last few days to be oblivious to the events there. The trial of Jesus before Pilate, the mobs pining for a guilty verdict, the vicious flogging, the death march to Golgotha, the execution by the remorseless Romans—not even the simplest of simpletons could be unaware of these facts.

Who is this man who seems to be so out of touch with events

that have devastated the hopes of Jews throughout Jerusalem? It is this question, or something like it, that recurs often in our accounts of human grief—whether in literature, film, music, philosophy, or religion—as we ponder the larger meaning of it all. Where is God in all our grief? What are we to make of our loss, and of our lives, as a result?

A work of fiction, considered the oldest story in the world, is driven along by exactly these questions. It is *Gilgamesh*, the tale of a king who reigned in the Mesopotamian city of Uruk (modern-day Iraq) in about 2750 BC.[15] The king has an intimate friend, Enkidu, a wild man who becomes civilized under his influence. He joins Gilgamesh in his many crusades, helping him defeat an assortment of monsters. But partly as a result of the king's imprudence, Enkidu is stricken in battle, and he senses from a dream that death is upon him.

Gilgamesh is desperate for a saving cure. "Now I will pray to the great gods for help, I will pray to Shamash and to your god . . . I will beg them to show you mercy, then I will have a gold statue made in your image. Don't worry, dear friend, you will soon get better, this votive image will restore you to health."[16]

Enkidu knows better. "There is no gold statue that can cure this illness, beloved friend," he says. "My fate is settled. There is nothing you can do."[17]

Death claims Enkidu, but Gilgamesh is seized by his own moment of magical thinking. The king is a fierce warrior, a man who has witnessed—and caused—many deaths in his lifetime. Yet now he can hardly admit what lay before his eyes, the lifeless body of his dearest friend in the world. "O Enkidu, what is this sleep that has seized you, that has darkened your face and stopped your breath?"[18] Gilgamesh is nearly overcome with grief.

Author and translator Stephen Mitchell calls Gilgamesh's lament "one of the most beautiful elegies in literature." In it, Gilgamesh invites an audience from both the natural and supernatural worlds to join him in mourning his friend:

> Hear me, elders, hear me, young men,
> my beloved friend is dead, he is dead,
> my beloved brother is dead, I will mourn
> as long as I breathe, I will sob for him
> like a woman who has lost her only child . . . [19]

The death of Enkidu changes the course of the king's life. He relinquishes his royal privileges; his days as warrior and king are over. Now he is a searcher, taking his first steps down his own Emmaus road. Gilgamesh leaves Uruk and embarks on a quest for wisdom, an anxious journey to the borders of the known world.

These are themes that cultures and civilizations—across continents and across the centuries—cannot seem to get out of their collective minds.

It was the realization of suffering and grief, in fact, that gave birth to one of the world's major religions. Buddhism begins with a solitary man, left bewildered by sorrow at discovering human frailty for the first time. Siddhartha Gautama was born around 563 BC, in modern-day Nepal, into wealth and nobility, shielded from the pains and unpleasantness of life. But then, as legend has it, he caught a glimpse of sickness, old age, and death. The experience produced a crisis of identity: How are we to live in a world full of such wretchedness? "Life is subject to age and death. Where is the realm of life in which there is neither age nor death?"[20]

Like Gilgamesh, Siddhartha rejects his worldly status,

leaving behind even his wife and infant son, and sets out to find an answer. Six years later, after sitting down under a fig tree to meditate, he awakens from a dream of suffering. His conclusion: the cause of all human misery is *tanha*, or desire. If we wish to be free of our pain and sorrow, we must not simply restrain our desires, our attachments, and our lusts. We must eliminate them. Along this path, he proclaims, is the way toward *nirvana*, which means, literally, to extinguish or blow out.

Thus, an experience of suffering produces one of the world's most radical responses in religion or philosophy: we remove suffering by extinguishing virtually all of our ordinary earthly desires. In the process, we free ourselves from all worldly entanglements. "Let, therefore, no man love anything," says the Buddha. "Those who love nothing and hate nothing, have no fetters." This is the path of enlightenment, the only way to be released from the cycle of birth, suffering, death, and rebirth. "And this is the noble truth of the stopping of sorrow," proclaims the Buddhist scripture. "It is the complete stopping of that craving."[21]

The Sadness Shield

We all seem to need a strategy for coping with the experience of grief. In the screen adaptation of Maurice Sendak's classic children's book *Where the Wild Things Are* (2009), we follow the adventures of Max, an imaginative child who feels neglected by his mother and older sister. He escapes into a fantastical world of hairy, monstrous creatures. Once these "wild things" threaten to devour him, Max pretends to possess magical powers and manages to convince the monsters to make him their king.

The creatures come to believe that Max has been sent to abolish suffering in their world and to establish permanent peace and happiness. And so they ask him: "Will you keep out all the sadness?" Still playacting his role as king and miracle worker, Max declares: "I have a sadness shield that keeps out all the sadness, and it's big enough for all of us."

Wouldn't we all like to have a sadness shield, to chase away all our grief and sorrow?

Contrary to the pabulum that often flows from the modern pulpit, the Bible never comes close to offering us a sadness shield. No religious text, no work of philosophy, no documentary film—no piece of literature or art is more sober about the problem of suffering and grief than the Bible. At the same time, the Christian attitude is anything but fatalistic. In the teachings and example of Jesus, we find an approach to human suffering that brings together the qualities of realism and hope.

Before we explore it, let's mention the popular alternatives. There are some who have given up on the idea of a Creator who is intimately involved in our lives. Their "watchmaker" view of God explains the persistence of suffering this way: God may have made the world, but after that he simply lost interest; we're left alone to fend for ourselves. There are others who basically tell us that heartache is a normal part of life and that we need to "embrace our pain," which brings to mind Eastern mystics who lie down on a bed of nails and invite some beefy bystander to jump up and down on their chests.

Still there are others, speaking as representatives of Christianity, whose approach to evil and suffering actually amounts to a different kind of denial. They insist that everything—literally, every action and reaction—happens according to God's prearranged plan. For them, there is no reason to grieve over anything or anyone. God has determined every event in our lives and in our world. Our job is not to pout but to get with the program.

In May 2001, for example, an influential evangelical pastor took to the pulpit to comment on a recent tragedy that was making international news. The Peruvian air force had mistakenly opened fire on a plane carrying an American missionary family, killing the mother and her seven-month-old daughter. The pastor announced, without a trace of self-doubt, that a "sovereign bullet" had taken their lives. God himself, we were assured, had orchestrated their deaths, down to the last lethal detail. Yes, God was the triggerman. Thus, there was no mystery to ponder, no need to shed tears for the departed.

We are all familiar with the pious refrain from a priest or minister, intended as consolation in the face of tragedy and loss: "It is God's will." What exactly do they mean? How in the world can they be so sure? Can this really be the teaching of Jesus about the nature of all human suffering? People who talk this way remind me of that recurring line from the petulant pharaoh of Egypt, deliciously played by Yul Brynner, in the movie *The Ten Commandments*. The pharaoh announces every imperial edict, whatever its dreary consequences, with a heart of stone: "So it is written, so it shall be done."

The Massacre of the Innocents

These are deep waters. The most probing of authors and intellects have drawn back from offering final answers. Political theorist Hannah Arendt, who covered the trial of Nazi war criminal

Erich Eichmann, wrote of the "perplexity of radical evil." Arthur Conan Doyle, speaking through his famous detective, Sherlock Holmes, often turned philosophical. "What is the object of this circle of misery and violence and fear?" Holmes asks solemnly in *The Adventure of the Cardboard Box*. "It must have a purpose, or else our universe has no meaning, which is unthinkable. But what purpose? That is humanity's great problem, to which reason, so far, has no answer."[22]

The authors of the Bible likewise considered this humanity's great problem. They, too, suggested that there are only partial answers in this life to the problem of suffering; we come to the limits of our intellect. Nevertheless, at least one truth stands out clearly. No matter how exalted our view of God, the moment we make him the author of evil is the moment we drag him down to our level—and worse. What we find in the faith of Jesus is something unexpected: a combination of realism and empathy toward human grief.

Consider the Old Testament leader Jeremiah, known as "the weeping prophet." There was a lot to cry about in his day. The Jewish people were experiencing intense suffering after being overwhelmed by the Babylonian Empire. Their leaders were dead, their temple was desecrated, their holy city was plundered, their women and children were carted off as captives by a foreign army. Most everyone was struggling to stay alive. The entire nation, according to Jeremiah, was in bitter anguish: "This is why I weep and my eyes overflow with tears. No one is near to comfort me, no one to restore my spirit. My children are destitute because the enemy has prevailed."[23]

Things are hardly any rosier in the New Testament. It is easy to miss the fact that the account of the birth of Jesus—romanticized with snowy night scenes and cooing manger animals—includes a wrenching story of ruthlessness and lethal violence.

Remember King Herod? He knew enough Jewish prophecy to suspect that the newborn babe in Bethlehem, already creating a local stir, might be the one destined to lead Israel. A vicious and paranoid man, Herod had no qualms about what had to be done: the child must die. To avoid any possibility that the baby might escape execution, Herod issued an open-ended death warrant. "And he gave orders to kill all the boys in Bethlehem and its vicinity who were two years old and under."[24] No potential rival to his throne would be permitted to live.

I have been attending Christian churches for nearly thirty years, and I must ask the question: Why is this story so rarely told from our pulpits or in our Christmas pageants?

Believers celebrate the birth of Jesus with hymns such as "Joy to the World," but there was overwhelming sorrow at this event as well. Imagine the scene: Word of Herod's order has spread like a plague throughout the city, as terrified families wait behind locked doors for the sound of Roman soldiers. The soldiers burst in, search for the male babies, seize them from their mothers' arms—and thrust a sword through their tiny bodies. How many children died that day in Bethlehem? How many mothers and fathers collapsed from grief?

Seventeenth-century artists such as Peter Paul Rubens graphically captured "The Massacre of the Innocents" on canvas because they understood that it was the tragic backdrop to the entire story. In this sense, they are better guides to the biblical account than many modern preachers. For the authors of the Bible took the problem of suffering seriously. They laid bare the doubts and the anguish of their subjects while refusing to offer pat answers or cheap comfort. In the gospel of Matthew, for example, we are told that the massacre at Bethlehem was an event predicted by the Jewish prophets, who understood something about the depth of human suffering:

> A voice is heard in Ramah,
>   weeping and great mourning,
> Rachel weeping for her children
>   and refusing to be comforted,
> because they are no more.[25]

For believers, the Christmas story brings promises of "peace on earth" and "tidings of great joy." Later on we'll see how the meaning of this event unlocks a world literally drenched in joy. But for now it's important to remember that in this very same story there is profound grief that cannot be consoled.

The God Who Suffers with Us

Herein lies one of the most compelling aspects of the life and teaching of Jesus: moral clarity about the problem of evil. Here, at last, is a religious teacher who identifies with the sufferings of others in the depths of his own soul.

The gospels tell the story of a man stricken with leprosy who approaches Jesus when he is teaching in one of the towns outside Jerusalem.[26] A disease that has terrified humanity since antiquity, leprosy remains a health problem even today in many parts of the developing world. We don't know how severe the man's condition was, but the disease can disfigure the skin and bones, and twist the limbs, fingers, and toes. If it affects a person's face, the nose can collapse, as if mashed with a hammer.

The psychological effects of the disease, though, would have been far worse than the physical effects. Luke's gospel tells us the man was "covered with leprosy."[27] In Jesus' day, Jewish law and custom would have insisted that the victim be completely cut off from his community; his illness was considered grave, infectious, and incurable. At some point in Jewish tradition, attitudes toward leprosy were driven less by health concerns than by moral censure. To be a leper was to be a person under God's wrath, guilty of some gross sin. And to associate with such a person—let alone to touch him—was to implicate one-self in his guilt.

A man in this condition might live for years without ever being touched by another human being. No wonder the leper "fell with his face to the ground" and begged Jesus to heal him. His life was awash in sorrow. "If you are willing," he pleaded, "you can make me clean."[28]

What will Jesus do? We are told that he is "filled with com-passion" at the sight of this man. The word *compassion* means "to suffer with." Let's make no mistake about it: Jesus is not some detached deity out of Greek mythology. He knows how to enter into another man's suffering. He refuses to be a stranger to human weakness. Instead, Jesus allows himself to be caught up in the struggles of a sick, solitary, desolate human being.

And then he acts, instinctively and without hesitation. "Jesus reached out his hand and touched the man." In this act, he breaks all social conventions to bring the man hope and heal-ing. "I am willing," he says. "Be clean!"[29] The man is cured of his leprosy on the spot. Thus, Jesus not only restored the man's physical health, but reintroduced the idea that God, in spite of it all, had not abandoned him.

Unlike other philosophers or religious teachers, Jesus treats evil and suffering as *invaders* in the world. They are experiences alien to the human person, fundamentally unnatural, and at war with the world God has made.[30]

Nowhere is this idea more plainly illustrated than in the story of Jesus at the tomb of his friend Lazarus, who had died a few days before he arrived on the scene. The account in John's gospel tells us repeatedly—three times, to be exact—that as he approached the gathering of mourners, Jesus became angry. One of the words used is the Greek term for "furious indignation." What exactly was Jesus angry about? Isn't death just a marvelous portal to another existence? Isn't terminal illness like a cheerful tour guide, gently taking us by the hand into paradise?

Not to Jesus. He came face-to-face with the death of a friend. He was confronted by grieving friends and family members. And he was deeply offended. As he saw it, the world God created good and beautiful and whole was desperately broken and in ruins. Jesus will act—incredibly—to restore Lazarus to life. But his first response—his reflex response—is anger. He was outraged, as well as grieved, by what sin and evil have done to destroy human lives.

"Where have you laid him?" he asked.

"Come and see, Lord," they replied.

It is not only anger that moved him, though. The account in John suggests that the scene of grief summoned a great reservoir of compassion. Thus we read: "Jesus wept."[31] In other words, Jesus' response to human suffering was never indifference or grim fatalism. It was, rather, a mix of grief, anger, and compassion.

This may come as a shock to the churchgoers among us, but Jesus grappled with the tragic events in our world and the suffering they bring. He understood how darkness could overcome the human heart as it succumbed to doubt and disbelief. Indeed, he once warned his followers that those who disregarded the truths that God had shown them—for whatever reason—would not prevail in their journey: "In the time of testing they fall away."[31]

Abandonment and Hope

Perhaps this is the greatest temptation in the experience of grief: to feel abandoned, either by God or the universe or whatever force it is we believe makes life worth living. In the end, we run the risk of abandoning God.

In Cormac McCarthy's novel *The Road*, we follow the struggle of a father and son to survive in a postapocalyptic world. They walk alone through a ravaged landcape, where the sky is always dark, the snow is gray, and it is cold enough "to crack the stones."[32] They have nothing but the clothes they are wearing and a cart of scavenged food. They are headed for the coast but have little reason to believe that life will be any more tolerable there.

At one point the father begins to think that death will finally take them, and he is nearly overcome with sadness. "There were times when he sat watching the boy sleep that he would begin to sob uncontrollably but it wasn't about death," McCarthy writes. "He wasn't sure what it was about but he thought it was about beauty or about goodness. Things he'd no longer any way to think about at all."[33] Life seemed so bereft of any sign of beauty or goodness that the absence of these gifts brought the deepest sorrow.

Quite often, it seems, the experience of great loss leads to skepticism, even cynicism about God and the world he has made. The Greek historian Thucydides, writing about a deadly plague that swept through Athens in 431 BC, describes a kind of moral chaos at work:

> For the catastrophe was so overwhelming that men, not knowing what would happen next to them, became indifferent to every rule of religion or of law. . . . No fear of god or law of man had a restraining influence. As for the gods, it seemed to be the same thing whether one worshipped them or not, when one saw the good and the bad dying indiscriminately.[34]

Are we really so different from the Greeks? About a year after the 9/11 attacks, PBS aired a documentary called *Faith and Doubt at Ground Zero*. Reporters interviewed survivors, ministers, rescue workers, and public intellectuals. The program was thick with doubt, anger, and resignation. "I couldn't believe that the God I talked to for thirty-five years . . . could turn this loving man into bones," a woman said. "I can't bring myself to speak to him anymore because I feel so abandoned," said another. A survivor seemed to speak for many when she admitted: "I look at him now as a barbarian . . . I think I'm a good Christian, but I have a different image of him now."[35]

By the end of Joan Didion's book *The Year of Magical Thinking*, there seems to be no room for thoughts of God or the hope of any ultimate comfort. The Scripture teaches us that God is mindful even of the sparrows in the forest. But as Didion sees it,

"There is no eye on the sparrow." Many of her contemporaries—writers, philosophers, artists, even theologians—have reached the same existential conclusion.

We may wonder whether the two friends on the road to Emmaus entertained a similar idea. *"He asked them, 'What are you discussing together as you walk along?' They stood still, their faces downcast."* Perhaps the thought that seizes them at this moment is not merely that Jesus was not their promised Messiah—but that there is no Messiah after all because there is no God in heaven to send him.

Nevertheless, grief becomes for many people the catalyst for a spiritual journey: deep sorrow can turn its victims into searchers. In *Gilgamesh*, the intensity of the king's sadness over the death of Enkidu is soon displaced by an equally intense desire for answers. His mourning creates within him an unshakable sense of his own mortality:

> Must I die too? Must I be as lifeless
> as Enkidu? How can I bear this sorrow
> that gnaws at my belly, this fear of death
> that restlessly drives me onward? If only
> I could find the one man whom the gods made immortal,
> I would ask him how to overcome death.[36]

Writing shortly after the 9/11 attacks, *Time* magazine's Lance Morrow explored the problem of evil in contemporary life. His book *Evil: An Investigation* cautions against demanding answers to all the many awful events in our world.

Morrow argues that quite often the answers we seek are not immediately available—and that this is true not only of the problem of evil and suffering, but of many other areas of human experience. No one knows exactly why a marriage fails or why a relationship ends in tears. But we don't give up on the idea of love or of lifelong friendships. Likewise, Morrow asks, do we abandon the effort to understand anything about God because we cannot understand this one great thing before our minds? "The world is not like that . . . We do not understand because a lot of things in the world are very hard to understand, but we keep trying anyway. We do not have the privilege of throwing up our hands."[37]

Christian leaders, at their best, have understood the great challenge that suffering presents to our mortal lives. They have tried to suffer with others in their sorrow and to help them live with unresolved questions in the midst of grief. Even by the end of his book *A Grief Observed*, C. S. Lewis makes no claim to have found answers to his most wrenching questions about suffering and death. But what he does gain—or recover—is a sense of confidence that God remains committed to him, to bless him. "God has not been trying an experiment on my faith or love in order to find out their quality," he writes. "He knew it already. It was I who didn't . . . He always knew that my temple was a house of cards."[38]

Martin Luther, the renegade monk who launched the Protestant Reformation, also set off a revolution in the medieval concept of the family by marrying an apostate nun, Katherine, and rejoicing in the blessings of family life. Yet he was no stranger to suffering. Historian Roland Bainton describes the scene when one of Luther's daughters, fourteen-year-old Magdalena, fell gravely ill.

Luther prayed, "O God, I love her so, but thy will be done." And turning to her, "*Magdalenchen*, my little girl, you would like to stay with your father here, and you would be glad to go to your Father in heaven?"

And she said, "Yes, dear father, as God wills."

And Luther reproached himself, because God had blessed him as no bishop had been blessed in a thousand years, and yet he could not find it in his heart to give God thanks. Katie stood off, overcome by grief; and Luther held the child in his arms as she passed on.

When she was laid away, he said, "*Du liebes Lenchen*, you will rise and shine like the stars and the sun. How strange it is to know that she is at peace and all is well, and yet to be so sorrowful!"[39]

The desire to find meaning in the blackest moments of our lives seems to be an intrinsic part of our nature; we can't really let go of the quest. The Christian faith, the faith according to Jesus, does not promise us immediate answers to all our most agonizing questions. We will not be given unwavering belief. We will not—in this life—find the comfort that we seek. There is no sadness shield.

But as we will see, there is the promise of something far better—if we do not give up the search for goodness in the valley of our grief.

3

The Poison of Religion

"He was a prophet, powerful in word and
deed before God and all the people. The
chief priests and our rulers handed him
over to be sentenced to death, and they
crucified him."

———◦∘◦———

*It is Friday afternoon, October 27, 1553, and a Spaniard named
Michael Servetus is tied to a stake on a hill just outside the gates of
Geneva, waiting to be executed.*

*Servetus is a talented physician, the first European to explain pul-
monary circulation, the movement of blood away from the heart to the
lungs. Skilled in biblical languages, he is also something of a theologian.
He is an opinionated man, often pugnacious, and it is his religious
opinions that have gotten him into trouble.*

*Servetus doesn't agree with Church teachings about the Trinity:
that there is one God, but that he exists as three persons—Father, Son,
and Holy Spirit. He has published several unorthodox writings on the
topic, which have incensed Church authorities; he seemed to be goading*

them into a fight. The Catholic Inquisitions in Spain and France have tried to arrest him for heresy. Protestant authorities in Geneva, led by John Calvin, want his head on a platter—literally.

"When religion is shaken to the core," Calvin warns, "when God is blasphemed in a most loathsome manner, when souls are led to perdition by godless and destructive teachings, then it is necessary to find the remedy which will prevent the deadly poison from spreading."[1] Many Church leaders, in fact, believed that the best remedy for the malignancy of men such as Servetus was execution.

For years Servetus lived as a hunted man. Even his brother, Juan, a priest, was sent to convince him to return to Spain for questioning. "I was sought up and down," Servetus writes, "to be snatched to my death."[2]

After escaping from a Catholic prison, Servetus makes the mistake of attending a Protestant church, where he is recognized instantly. He is arrested, tried, and found guilty of heresy, like thousands of others before him. He begs in vain to be killed by the sword instead of by fire. His last words: "Jesus, Son of the Eternal God, have mercy on me."

—————◆◆◆—————

Religious leaders have always worried about the poison of heresy, ideas that seem to deny or denigrate the faith. Yet there is another kind of poison, that of religious zeal gone wrong, what might be called the *poison of religion*. Much of the history of the West, and the world at large, has been tortured and debased by it. Maybe half of the wickedness in all the world is committed under its name. "Men never do evil so completely and cheerfully," observed Pascal, "as when they do it from religious conviction."[3]

On the Wrong Side of God

It was the poison of religion that, on a different Friday afternoon, claimed the life of another unorthodox troublemaker. His name was Jesus of Nazareth. There's no escaping the fact that the execution of Jesus—a good man, by nearly all accounts—was instigated by people of faith, by the Jewish authorities in Jerusalem. The Christian church, to its great shame, has used this fact as a reason to despise and persecute the Jews throughout history. That history aside, it is the involvement of the Jewish establishment in the death of Jesus that helps to throw our two companions into a state of near despair.

The "chief priests" among the Jews, after all, were not some rakish sect of extremists whom nobody took seriously. They were an elite group of religious leaders who could trace their family tree to the honored tribe of Levi, the only one of Israel's twelve tribes whose members could serve as priests. These men, and these men alone, were in charge of the temple in Jerusalem, the holiest site in ancient Israel. No one else could enter the temple or offer sacrifices to God to atone for the sins of their fellow Jews. They were among the most important and revered figures in Israel.

If you found yourself on the wrong side of the chief priests, you were on the wrong side of God.

So imagine the disciples' confusion. Just about everyone believed, as these men did, that Jesus was a prophet. In the Jewish world, that meant he was a man with a message from heaven, sent by God and protected by him in a special way. A prophet was a person "upon whom the Spirit of God rested."[4] He was given divine insight into God's plans and purposes.

Jesus appeared to be such a man. He was, as the disciples described him, *"powerful in word and deed before God and all the people."* They had experienced the force of his teaching many times. In packed synagogues they heard him describe the kindness and mercy of God toward those who seemed least deserving of it. They were among the thousands gathered on hillsides, families in tow, to hear him explain what it meant to be truly blessed in God's eyes. "Blessed are the poor in spirit," he said, "for theirs is the kingdom of heaven."[5] When he spoke, his words seemed to penetrate deep into their hearts and minds and summon them into another world.

The strength of his speech was matched by the power of his hands. No one had ever seen anything like it in Israel: a prophet who could heal people who had no right to hope for healing. With their own eyes they watched him cure the desperately sick, instantly, with a touch—people blind from birth, disfigured by disease, tormented by evil spirits. "Pick up your mat and walk," he told a helpless cripple.[6] And the man did! There was no one who came to Jesus with a need, no matter what their reputation or rank in society, who was not restored to health.

How could a man like that be on the wrong side of God?

It was not hard to see that many of the Jewish leaders felt threatened by Jesus' growing influence and popularity among the crowds. The disciples had seen him clash with the Scribes and Pharisees. More than once he took them to task for their cold legalisms. Even the Roman governor, Pontius Pilate, knew that "it was out of self-interest that they handed Jesus over to him."[7]

The truth of the matter is that Jesus unleashed his most withering criticism on the most outwardly religious people in society, people who lacked real faith, but used their pretend religion to impress or manipulate others. He called them "vipers," "white-washed tombs," "unmarked graves," and "children of the devil."[8] Our image of Jesus wearing a sedated smile and preaching a cream-puff morality—an exponent of "love" who never offended anyone—needs serious revision. Jesus offended lots of people, especially religious people. Nothing angered him more, in fact, than the poison of religion, the faith of the pious hypocrite.

That may come as a surprise to those who have walked away from the church because of its record of failure, abuse, and repression. They have more in common with the religion of Jesus than they might think.

Counterfeit Faith

Christianity—or, more accurately, the church acting in its name—has inspired an awful amount of human carnage. Many believers have failed to grasp just how far the church has drifted from the life and teachings of Jesus over the centuries. Skeptics seem acutely conscious of the divide. I was reminded of this fact years ago when I first saw the Woody Allen film *Hannah and Her Sisters* at a university theater. One of the characters in the film, a cynical artist, gets into a discussion with his lover about God: "If Jesus were to come back and see what people have done in his name, he'd throw up." The campus crowd erupted into applause.

So let us be frank, without being unkind, about the failures of contemporary Christianity. For all the talk about "new life" and "amazing grace," most Christians appear to be living their lives more or less like everybody else. Many, in fact, seem to be doing worse. "Too much of the good life ends up being toxic, deforming us spiritually," confessed author David Goetz in *Death by Suburb*. "The drive to succeed, and to make one's children succeed, overpowers the best intentions to live more reflectively, no matter the piety."[9]

By the poison of religion, I don't mean the problem of Christians who live safe, middle-class, unremarkable lives. The real danger is the pretend factor, the haze of religiosity that tries to conceal the shallowness—and the deepening rot underneath.

We know the telltale signs: thundering preachers who bilk their congregations to support their own lavish lifestyles; politicians who trumpet their Christian faith while cheating on their wives; church leaders obsessed with the sins of others but who can't imagine iniquity in their own tent. A church in Kansas, for example, eager to see America suffer divine wrath for its sins, famously deploys its members to military funerals with signs that read "Thank God for Dead Soldiers" and "You're Going to Hell."[10]

Or consider the crisis of child sexual abuse that has seized the Catholic Church for more than a decade. There seems to be no bottom to it. Even Pope Benedict XVI has been criticized for his role in the Church's failure to discipline abusive priests and remove them from ministry. The problem first arose in the United States, but thousands of similar cases of the sexual exploitation of children have been reported—from parishes in Ireland, Germany, Austria, the Netherlands, Switzerland, and Italy.

What has emerged is a pattern of institutional denial and cover-up. A Church commission in Dublin concluded that Catholic leaders were concerned only with avoiding scandal, protecting the reputation of the Church, and guarding its financial assets. Even as credible stories of abusive priests came to the attention of Church authorities, "the welfare of children, which should have been the first priority, was not even a factor to be considered."[11] Church leaders, rather than repentant, have been defensive. During a Good Friday service in St. Peter's Basilica, a senior Vatican priest even complained that attacks on the Church were like the history of persecution and "collective violence" against the Jews.[12]

What kind of religion, we are entitled to ask, puts the well-being of children at the bottom of its priority list? What kind of spiritual leadership condones the sexual exploitation of children and then claims the role of helpless victim?

"If ever the book which I am not going to write is written, it must be the full confession by Christendom of Christendom's specific contribution to the sum of human cruelty and treachery," writes C. S. Lewis. "Large areas of 'the World' will not hear us till we have publicly disowned much of our past."[13] Lewis might have added that we need to disavow much of the present as well.

The Spirit of the Inquisition

A good way to understand the present state of affairs, though, is to reflect for a moment on the past. We must try to understand the remarkable capacity of organized religion to produce outwardly devout individuals with hearts of greed and malice.

The great Catholic reformer Erasmus of Rotterdam brilliantly satirized the problem in his sixteenth-century blockbuster *The Praise of Folly*. Erasmus accused religious leaders of confusing their impenetrable speculations about God with real wisdom about holy living. At one point he poked fun at the elaborate headgear worn by professors of divinity, a status symbol denied to lesser mortals. "Don't be surprised when you see them at public disputations with their heads so carefully wrapped up in swaths of cloth," he wrote, "for otherwise they would clearly explode."[14]

This was one of many complaints against the Catholic Church during the Middle Ages, when the machinery of the Inquisition slipped into high gear. Church Inquisitors were neither the moral equivalent of the Nazis nor the bumbling clerics of Monty Python skits. They were ordinary men who unleashed atrocities in the name of God. Before it ran its course, the Inquisition robbed thousands of their property, sent thousands more to their deaths, and created a culture of fear and betrayal that threatened the entire social fabric of Europe. In a 2001 examination of clerical responsibility, Pope John Paul II called the Inquisition "a tormented phase in the history of the Church."[15]

Why does this legacy of shame matter to us today? Because the architects of the Inquisition did not set out to wreak such havoc. They were misled by the same spirit of hypocrisy that haunts contemporary religion.

Let's look at it briefly. Launched in the thirteenth century, the Catholic Inquisition was composed of a series of Church courts, spread throughout Europe, with one function: to root out and prosecute heresy. A heretic was a person who had accepted Christianity and was baptized, but promoted doctrines contrary to those upheld by the Church. From the Catholic perspective, the purpose of the Inquisition was pastoral. It sought, first, to lead the accused toward repentance and, second, to protect others from the danger that heresy created to their own spiritual lives. Whatever its motives, the Inquisition quickly became an instrument of terror leveled against all the perceived enemies of the Church.

The Spanish Inquisition, probably the most savage of all the Church Inquisitions, was set up in 1481 under the control of a Dominican friar, Tomás de Torquemada. He was known as "the hammer of heretics," and for good reason. In the first eight years of operation, "the hammer" struck down 700 people, all burned at the stake. He set the tone for the Church in Spain. By the 1540s, more than 20,200 people were executed, including Protestants, Muslims, and Jews. Torquemada was so hated that he traveled with a bodyguard of 50 mounted guards and 250 armed men.[16]

The onset of the Protestant Reformation—the spiritual revolution launched by Martin Luther in 1517—created thousands of dissenters from the Catholic Church almost immediately. From the Catholic standpoint, they were heretics who had to be confonted and overcome. Thus, the Roman Inquisition was set up in 1542, as the Church was composing its theological rebuttal to the Protestants at the Council of Trent.

Compared to Spain, the Roman Inquisition was less violent and systematic. There were fewer executions. Nevertheless, it was no pajama party; the same pattern of suspicion and persecution prevailed. Leaders such as Pope Paul IV made sure of it. As one Catholic historian has written, when Gian Pietro Carafa was named pope in May 1555, a "new harsh wind" blew through Rome. The Jesuit leader, Ignatius of Loyola, said that his bones quaked when he first learned of Carafa's election. "Even if my own father were a heretic," the new pope declared, "I would gather the wood to burn him."[17]

Historians debate the lethality of the Inquisition, but whatever the actual death toll, the blight on the Christian gospel remains. Ordinary people were spied upon, accused, harassed, arrested, and sent to the gallows for one reason: they failed to adhere to Church teaching and practice. Unlike the secular courts, the proceedings of the Inquisition were kept secret and the laws of evidence were often ignored. Whether falsely accused or not, thousands perished in the flames and tens of thousands were sent to prison. And it all proceeded in the name of Christian truth, under the authority of the highest officials of the Church.

What were the motives of the Inquisitors? No doubt some acted out of concern for spiritual truth, twisted as it was. But it is important to realize that the Inquisition was a self-financing institution, drawing on the property of the condemned. Church authorities thus created a financial incentive to secure convictions—hence the use of torture. Meanwhile, the surest route to advancement in the hierarchy was to prove your zeal to put down heresy. No man earned a cardinal's hat by showing mercy toward the godless.

Here is the poison of religion: the use of coercion and violence to serve the Will to Power, all under the pretense of piety.

The Inquisition finally petered out by the early nineteenth century. The last official Spanish execution for heresy was in 1826, when a schoolmaster was hanged for substituting "Praise be to God" in place of "Ave Maria" in school prayers.[18]

Dogma vs. Charity

What contributed to this long, black episode in the history of the Church? In a word, *dogma*. As the Church clarified and formalized its teaching, the list of doctrines and creeds multiplied—as did the number of heretics. Catholic thinkers such as Erasmus complained that the thirst for persecution had become insatiable. "Once faith was more a matter of a way of life than a profession of articles," he wrote. "Articles increased, but sincerity decreased: contention boiled over, charity grew cold."[19]

In other words, the Church became obsessed with correct doctrine rather than with the kind of life modeled by Jesus in the gospels. Protestant theologian Philip van Limborch, in his 1685 work *The History of the Inquisition*, criticized the Church for being led by "men of corrupt minds" and "strong prejudices." He declared that anyone unfamiliar with the teachings of Jesus in the gospels would look at the violence meted out by churchmen against their neighbors and come to one conclusion: Christianity "was one of the worst religions in the world."[20]

These habits of mind were not confined to the Catholic Church, of course. Protestants added more than their fair share to the record of militant religion. When Calvinists came to power in places such as Scotland or the Netherlands, violent crackdowns on religious dissent were the norm. It is hard to imagine today, but even the Anglican Church—known for its spirit of moderation—took a lead role in the Protestant campaigns of repression following the Reformation.

By 1660, when the Church of England was restored after the English Revolution, a new policy of intolerance was put in place: worship outside the official Anglican establishment became a criminal act. Virtually overnight, an entire subculture of dissenters, numbering in the tens of thousands, faced the threat of fines, arrests, and imprisonment. Ministers who failed to tow the line lost their livelihoods. Disobedience to the national church was seen as disloyalty to the Crown—an act of treason. "If Restoration England did not see a return to the burning of heretics," writes British historian John Coffey, "it did witness persecution on a grand scale."[21]

The pattern was repeated in other Protestant states—as was the problem of counterfeit religion. John Tillotson, an English minister often at odds with the Protestant establishment, described a kind of moral inversion at work: the deeper the void of spiritual life, the stronger the impulse to persecute others over differences of belief or practice. "It is very possible," he warned from the pulpit in 1694, "that Men may be devout and zealous in Religion, very nice and scrupulous about the worship and service of God; and yet because of their palpable defect in points of justice and honesty, of meekness and humility, of peace and charity, may be gross and odious hypocrites."[22]

The English philosopher John Locke, who read and admired Tillotson's sermons, based much of his famous appeal for religious liberty on the scandal of hypocritical religion. Locke's *A Letter Concerning Toleration* (1689) took aim at Protestant ministers who enlisted the gospel of Jesus only to treat others in ways that Jesus could not possibly condone. "At last it appears what zeal for the church, joined with the desire for dominion, is capable to produce," he wrote, "and how easily the pretence of religion, and of the care of souls, serves for a cloak to covetousness, rapine, and ambition."[23]

The problem of the "pretence of religion"—otherwise known as hypocrisy—is an old one. It was a frequent subject of the teachings of Jesus. He likened it to the tiniest of organisms, which nevertheless spreads and overwhelms its host. It was a condition to be avoided at all costs. "Be on your guard against the yeast of the Pharisees," he warned, "which is hypocrisy."[24]

Islam and the Terrorist Temptation

It is useful to keep this history in mind, especially as we consider the latest manifestation of the persecuting impulse in religion, the face of militant Islam.

Some examples of excessive zeal among Muslims border on the comical. Each year, just before Valentine's Day, religious police in Saudi Arabia crack down on the sale of flowers, jewelry, and candy. And they're not crazy about the color red either. Backed by the Commission for Promotion of Virtue and Prevention of Vice, they're on a mission from Allah to make sure no one celebrates the pagan holiday. Recently the national newspaper *Al-Riyadh* ran an article trying to discourage Cupid's Day with this curious claim: "A fifth of adults prefer to spend Valentine's Day with their pets instead of their partners."[25]

In her bestselling book *Infidel* (2007), Ayaan Hirsi Ali explains why she fled the culture of control that darkens the lives of Muslim women in her native Somalia. Forced marriages and genital mutilation are the norm; resistance means disgrace, banishment—or worse. For Ali and many of her friends, militant religion forced them into lives of deceit or despair. "Excision of my genitals didn't eliminate the human sex drive, and neither did the fear of hellfire," she writes. "Repression only led to hypocrisy and lying, strategies that corrupt the human individual."[26]

Honor killings—the murder of a family member by a

relative who believes the victim brought shame upon them—are not uncommon in the Middle East and other Muslim-majority countries. A few years ago in Pakistan, three teenage girls made headlines when they defied tribal elders and tried to arrange their own marriages in civil court. They were abducted, taken to a remote field, then beaten, shot, and buried alive. A Pakistani lawmaker actually justified the murders before Parliament. "These are centuries-old traditions and I will continue to defend them," said Israr Ullah Zehri. "Only those who indulge in immoral acts should be afraid."[27]

It does not seem to occur to these true believers that murdering another human being qualifies as an act of immorality.

In Turkey, the threat of an honor killing led a seventeen-year-old girl to attempt suicide three times. She had had an affair with a boy and was ordered by her uncle to take her own life and "clean our shame" or others would do the dirty work for her. "This region is religious and it is impossible to be yourself if you are a woman," she said. "You can either escape by leaving your family and moving to a town, or you can kill yourself."[28]

It sounds like a Shakespearean tragedy—live in exile or commit suicide. Is this really what the founder of Islam had in mind for his followers?

Yet this brand of abuse is child's play compared to the ideology of radical Islam that inspired the terrorist attacks of 9/11. The mastermind of those attacks, Osama bin Laden, said he was called "to follow in the footsteps of the Messenger and to communicate his message to all nations."[29] Even with the death of bin Laden, there seems to be no deficit of Muslim recruits to pick up where he left off. Moreover, the stated objectives of Al-Qaeda's global network have not changed: to eradicate all

Western influence from Muslim lands; forcibly convert or kill alleged infidels; impose Islamic law in every state that comes under their influence; and establish a theocratic dictatorship—a new caliphate—extending from Algeria to Indonesia.

If Christians resorted to sub-Christian tactics to accomplish their goals in an earlier century, radical Muslims have taken their rationalizing much further. They seem to delight in savagery and murder. Somehow, over the last ten years, we have gotten used to the idea of young men who blow themselves up at wedding ceremonies, who torture and dismember their victims, who set off bombs in mosques, who murder women for failing to wear a veil, who behead young girls on their way to school, who open fire on playgrounds and soccer stadiums—all in the name of religious purity.

The Pakistani terrorist Faisal Shahzad, who in 2010 tried to blow up Times Square in New York City, speaks for many of them. After being sentenced to life without parole, he remained defiant: "If I am given a thousand lives, I will sacrifice them all for the sake of Allah fighting this cause. . . . Consider me only a first droplet of the flood that will follow." Shahzad, who pleaded guilty to ten federal crimes, offered no regrets: "I'm happy with the deal that God has given me."[30]

How can men of such depraved indifference to human life be so certain that God is on their side? And what kind of deity makes a bargain sanctifying their barbarism? Of course, it is true that most Muslims reject violence and terrorism, and that in this they look to the example of Muhammad. They argue that he showed restraint toward his enemies and that he proclaimed mercy to be a fundamental attribute of God. Indeed, the idea of God's mercy announced by the Qur'an is embodied in the Muslim practice of beginning all important speeches or books with the phrase: "In the name of God, the Merciful and Compassionate."

Nevertheless, these outward trappings of piety do not change the facts on the ground. Virtually all the terrorist attacks against the West over the last decade have been committed by individuals invoking Islam and the Qur'an. They have found support for their deeds in the life and teachings of the Prophet. "If the peoples of the Middle East continue on their present path," writes Princeton scholar Bernard Lewis, "the suicide bomber may become a metaphor for the whole region, and there will be no escape from a downward spiral of hate."[31]

The poison of religion—the Will to Power concealed by the language of faith—is thriving within the body of Islam.

Does Religion Really Poison *Everything*?

No wonder the legacy of religious militancy and repression is a ripe target in popular culture these days. It is not easy to find in either literature or film a religious figure who is the protagonist *and* a likeable, honest, or even well-meaning person. Sister Aloysius Beauvier, Meryl Streep's character in the movie *Doubt*, seems more typical. The creepy and punitive principal of a New York Catholic school strikes terror in the hearts of virtually anything that moves. Reviewers dubbed her role "the Devil wears a habit."

Let's face it: the mendacious minister is a character we love to hate. This surely explains much of the success of novels such as Barbara Kingsolver's *The Poisonwood Bible*, whose main character, Baptist missionary Nathan Price, is a cardboard cutout of hypocritical religion. His single-minded zealotry all but destroys his family. "I could never work out whether we were to view religion as a life insurance policy or a life sentence," muses his daughter Leah. "I can understand a wrathful God who'd just as soon dangle us all from a hook. And I can understand a tender, unprejudiced Jesus. But I could never quite feature the two of them living in the same house."[32]

Vanity Fair columnist Christopher Hitchens, an atheist, gave up on God early in life and never looked back—not even after contracting terminal cancer. *God Is Not Great: How Religion Poisons Everything,* his polemical book, views virtually all religious belief as an obstacle to progress and rationality. "God did not create man in his own image," he wrote. "Evidently, it was the other way about, which is the painless explanation for the profusion of gods and religions, and the fratricide both between and among faiths, that we see all about us and that has so retarded the development of civilization."[33] Lots of people seem to agree with Hitchens, since the book sat on the *New York Times* bestseller list for weeks.

Skepticism is one thing. But cynicism about religious commitment—it works like a toxin in everything it touches—won't do for most of us. Yes, religion has been a collaborator in great evil. But people of faith also have been great liberators from the forces of tyranny and oppression. "In the opening chapter of the Hebrew Bible, God declares that He has made man in His own image: to teach us that one who is not in my image is still in God's image," writes Jonathan Sacks, Britain's chief rabbi. "That is the most powerful antidote to hate ever created."[34]

History bears out that judgment. The very idea of religious freedom, for example, was developed and championed not by leaders of the secular Enlightenment, but by Christian ministers, theologians, and philosophers. Christians such as Sebastian Castellio, armed with the Bible, clashed openly with John Calvin over the execution of Servetus. "When the Genevans killed Servetus," he said, "they did not defend a doctrine, they killed a man." Persecution, he insisted, was an affront to the ethics of Jesus and to the moral implications of his gospel: "When I examine my own life I see so many and such great sins that I do not think I could even obtain pardon from my Savior if I were thus ready to condemn others."[35] Believers such as John Goodwin, Jeremy Taylor, William Penn, Roger Williams, and Philip van Limborch argued passionately that coercion in matters of faith violated the example and teachings of Jesus.

Even John Locke, considered the father of political liberalism, saw Christianity as the great ally of the rights of conscience. It was the Christian gospel, Locke argued, that supplied the moral bedrock for natural rights and political freedoms. The problem, he said, was not religion, but rather a *deficit of authentic faith.* "If the Gospel and the apostle may be credited," he wrote in *A Letter Concerning Toleration*, "no man can be a Christian without charity, and without the faith which works, not by force, but by love."[36] Locke's biblical argument for toleration helped enshrine the rights of conscience in the political constitutions of the West.

Is this the religion that poisons everything?

When nearly all of European society justified the enslavement of human beings, trading and transporting men, women, and children like cattle, a young politician stood up in the parliament of a great nation and said "enough." His forty-year campaign against the African slave trade made him one of the most despised men of his day. "I mean not to accuse anyone," he told his fellow lawmakers, "but to take the shame upon myself, in common indeed with the whole Parliament of Britain, for having suffered this horrid trade to be carried on under their authority."[37]

William Wilberforce, an evangelical with a passion for social justice, took on the slave trade of an empire and prevailed.

Is this the religion that poisons everything?

When the long, black shadow of fascism fell upon a continent, when the racist fury of the Nazis announced its hatred of Jews and of the God they worshipped, a young Lutheran minister found that he could not remain silent. Convinced that the gospel of Jesus commanded his followers to stand up for the oppressed, he spoke up for the Jews and the infinite worth of every human being under heaven. Dietrich Bonhoeffer left the safety of an academic post and joined a plot to assassinate Adolf Hitler.

Why did he do it? Because Christians were called not only to "bandage the victims under the wheel" of oppression, he said, but "to put a spoke in the wheel itself."[38] Bonhoeffer was exposed, imprisoned, and executed by the Nazis.

Is this the religion that poisons everything?

The same spirit of tenacity and conviction has guided nearly all the great reform movements against injustice in the West. They found inspiration and support in the teachings of the Bible.

Honest skeptics have acknowledged the redemptive influence of religion. A century ago, William James, the Harvard psychologist and agnostic, stunned his colleagues with his critique of Christian belief in *The Varieties of Religious Experience* (1903). Prior to James, no scholar had given such attention to the process—and the effects—of religious conversion. His basic argument was that there is something authentic and profoundly beneficial about faith commitment. "The best fruits of religious experience are the best things history has to show," he wrote. "The highest flights of charity, devotion, trust, patience, bravery to which the wings of human nature have spread themselves have been flown for religious ideals."[39]

It is true that James showed little patience for traditional religion, what he called "the spirit of dogmatic dominion." Yet he confessed to being deeply impressed by believers whose experience of God launched them into acts of service and sacrifice. "St. Paul made our ancestors familiar with the idea that every soul is virtually sacred," he wrote. "The saints, with their extravagance of human tenderness, are the great torch-bearers of this belief, the tip of the wedge, the clearers of the darkness."[40]

What Holiness Looks Like

The point that must not be missed is that the Bible is utterly realistic about the poison of religion. Jesus was no fool about human nature. He was well aware of our inclination to abuse religion for our own selfish ends.

Consider an encounter that Jesus had at the home of a religious leader, a Pharisee, named Simon. As was the custom, Jesus and Simon were sitting on the floor, reclining at a table as lunch was being served. Suddenly, a woman—delicately described as someone who "lived a sinful life" in town—made a surprise appearance. In other words, a known prostitute walked into the equivalent of the High and Holy Tabernacle on Bible Belt Boulevard. It was scandalous. Yet there she stood, beside Jesus, overcome with emotion. There were no words to say. All she could do was weep.

Why was she weeping? Perhaps because one morning this woman wandered into the crowds around the Teacher, and as she listened to him speak, she was filled with regret. But not only regret, for there was hope in his message, and something he said stirred her. "It is not the healthy who need a doctor, but the sick," Jesus said. "For I have not come to call the righteous, but sinners."[41] If God is really anything like this, she thought, maybe there was a chance for her to start over, to put things right. So she broke all conventions and entered a fortress of religious rectitude, the house of a Pharisee.

As soon as she saw Jesus, her tears flowed so freely that they soaked his feet. She wiped his feet with her hair, kissed them, and poured perfume over them from a bottle she brought with her.

Simon could hardly contain himself. The scornful look said it all: "If this man were a prophet, he would know who is touching him and what kind of woman she is—that she is a sinner."[42] In the sanctified cocoon of the religious professional, prophets and prostitutes don't eat at the same lunch buffet. This man, Jesus, was clearly on the wrong side of God.

But Jesus understood the holiness of God much differently than Simon. To help him grasp it, he told a story about two men in debt to a moneylender. One man's loan was fifty times the size of the other's—yet the moneylender canceled both their debts. "Now which of them will love him more?" Jesus asked. Simon replied, somewhat grudgingly: "I suppose the one who had the bigger debt forgiven."[43]

Here again we see how religion can operate like a cancer in the bloodstream. As a Pharisee, a stickler about observing every rule in the Jewish law, Simon had lots of theology under his belt. But he suffered from a deficit of faith; he lacked a heart of gratitude for the kindness God had shown him in his own life. As he dressed himself in the robes and rituals of religion, his self-image skyrocketed. Yet the more he approached faith as a public pose, as a performance act, the more his soul withered. As Abraham Heschel once observed, "Hypocrisy rather than heresy is the cause of spiritual decay."[44]

Thus, in Simon's cynical eyes, the wayward woman was not just an irreligious person; she was a contemptible person, deserving only to be judged, despised, and marginalized.

Simon's spiritual condition was like the *Hindenburg* airship in the early evening hours of May 6, 1937. It was a majestic sight, soaring at 650 feet, high above it all, its passengers cozily unaware of the messy distractions below. The zeppelin offered astonishing luxury: fine food, a baby grand piano, breathtaking views. As one passenger described the ride: "You feel as though you are carried in the arms of angels."[45] At 7:25 p.m., as the airship prepared to land at the Lakehurst Naval Air Station in New Jersey, a small flame appeared on the top of the tail section of the vessel. Within thirty four seconds, the massive blimp was engulfed in flames and burned to the ground.

Jesus made it his business to bring down the spiritual blimps of his day. Now it was Simon's turn. "You did not give me any water for my feet," Jesus told him, "but she wet my feet with her tears and wiped them with her hair. You did not give me a kiss, but this woman, from the time I entered, has not stopped kissing my feet. . . . Therefore, I tell you, her many sins have been forgiven—as her great love has shown. But whoever has been forgiven little loves little."[46]

Hence the paradox: the prostitute knew more about the grace of God than the priest.

The founder of Christianity was never naïve about how religion could corrupt the human heart. He knew it could insulate a man from the truth about himself. Wrongly understood, religion divorces the believer from human need. His doctrine deadens him to the qualities of mercy, empathy, and humility. As his inward soul shrivels, he resorts more and more to the lifeless mechanics of religion. Pilgrimages, rituals, relics, and creeds begin to multiply. Meanwhile, love and compassion—born out of gratefulness to God—begin to fade. "Whoever has been forgiven little loves little."

Part of the genius of Jesus the teacher was his knowing how to expose the problem. More than once he pushed people toward a crisis moment, as he did the Pharisee. The political revolutionary Thomas Paine called moments like these "touchstones of sincerity and hypocrisy." They are encounters with reality that "sift out the hidden thoughts of man" and "bring things and men to light, which might otherwise have lain forever undiscovered."[47]

The travelers on the road to Emmaus have found themselves in the midst of such an encounter, and in their conversation with a stranger we overhear their hidden thoughts. *"He was a prophet, powerful in word and deed before God and all the people. The chief priests and our rulers handed him over to be sentenced to death, and they crucified him."* How could their spiritual teachers believe they were doing the will of God? How could they condemn Jesus to die as a criminal? It was like condemning goodness itself.

Only false religion, poisoned religion, could behave this way.

4

The End of Illusions

"But we had hoped that he was the one who
was going to redeem Israel."

———————◆———————

In his bestselling book Into the Wild, *Jon Krakauer tells the true
story of Christopher McCandless, a young man from a wealthy East
Coast family who leaves home and gives away all his possessions to
plunge into the Alaskan wilderness "in search of raw, transcendent
experience."[1] What first launches this man on his journey, though,
has nothing to do with the thrill of discovery. It is, rather, the pain
of discovery that sends him searching.*

*After graduating high school, McCandless learns that his parents
had lied to him about their relationship all his life. His mother was
his father's mistress, an accomplice in a tale of deceit and denial that
wrecked a marriage and poisoned family relationships. McCandless
is an illegitimate child. Unable to forgive his father's mistakes or the
attempt to hide them, his anger ripens. The knowledge of his father's
deception becomes, in the words of his sister, Carine, "a murder of
every day's truth." It is intolerable. "He felt his whole life turn, like*

a river suddenly reversing the direction of its flow, suddenly running uphill," she says. "These revelations struck at the core of Chris's sense of identity. They made his entire childhood seem like fiction."

The story was adapted to the screen in the 2007 film Into the Wild, *directed by Sean Penn. McCandless has the soul of a naturalist, a do-gooder, an adventurer, a seeker. He is a young man filled with idealism, yet driven by a river of rage underneath. His anger, it seems, causes him to sever his ties not only with family but with civilization itself. Ultimately, it overwhelms his common sense. McCandless shrugs off warnings that he is heading into treacherous terrain completely ill prepared: "I won't run into anything I can't deal with on my own."[2]*

A ferocious sense of disillusionment sends Christopher McCandless into the Alaskan wild north of Mt. McKinley in April 1992. Four months later, in a remote stretch of woods, a party of moose hunters discovers his decomposed body.

———◦•◦———

There is something about the spectacle of dreams destroyed that fixes our gaze, almost irresistibly. We feel compelled, against our better instincts, to watch the horrid scene unfold, like motorists slowing to catch a glimpse of a car wreck. "Rob the average man of his life-illusion," wrote Henrik Ibsen, "and you rob him of his happiness at the same stroke."[3]

Perhaps this is what drew many onlookers to the execution of Jesus at the hands of Roman soldiers. No one in Israel's collective memory stirred the hopes of Jews as he had. No one spoke so movingly about God's relentless love for his chosen people, or so convincingly about God's triumph over his enemies. In the kingdom of heaven, he said, there were no seats reserved for the rich and powerful. Rather, it was the humble who could expect an inheritance, a place of peace and safety and blessing. This is the vision that attracted the two disciples, and many like them, to the Teacher from Nazareth.

Yet now, at the scene of his death, all his magnificent words have dissolved into the putrid air of Golgotha. This man of peace, this champion of the weak, had confronted the most powerful men in Jerusalem—and lost everything in the contest. "He saved others," an onlooker taunted, "but he can't save himself."[4]

The shock of his failure instantly transforms his inner circle of disciples. Once devoted foot soldiers in a religious revolution, they devolve into frightened and demoralized fugitives. Most of them, for fear of arrest, avoid completely the scene of Jesus' execution. A few watch from a distance; others scramble for a safe house and lock the doors behind them. Others, like Cleopas and his companion, flee the city altogether. A sense of disbelief—of disillusionment—engulfs them like a suffocating blackness, as if they are doomed to live all their waking lives without the hope of daylight.

Who, if anyone, can be trusted?

The Illusions We Live By

At this point in the story it is reasonable to wonder whether the collapse of their faith was perfectly predictable—and long overdue.

The followers of Jesus, some would say, were revolutionary

romantics. They dreamed of a society where peace and fellowship were the rule. Call it a religious variety of John Lennon's fantastical vision: a world that has done away with war, greed, and hunger. "Imagine . . . a brotherhood of man."

Didn't Jesus encourage this same impossible ideal by talking repeatedly about the arrival of the kingdom of heaven?

We've heard these musings before in human societies. The ancient Sumerians dreamed of a place where "the bird of death did not utter the cry of death, the lion did not devour, the wolf did not tear the lamb . . . there was no widow, no sickness, no old age, no lamentation."[5] Plato gave this society a political twist in his *Republic*, in which a perfect state is ruled by men endowed with unfailing justice. Thomas More, a devout Catholic, took the genre of the ideal society to a new level with his provocative work *Utopia*. In More's imagination, people would order their lives so that "everyone gets a fair share, so there are never any poor men or beggars. Nobody owns anything, but everyone is rich—for what greater wealth can there be than cheerfulness, peace of mind, and freedom from anxiety?"[6]

The society these followers of Jesus sought to bring about, we are told, was like these utopian societies. It was just as placid, sublime, compelling—and illusory. It was destined to end in failure.

For many skeptics, *illusion* is the operative word. Following the work of Sigmund Freud, modern thinkers tend to view religious belief as a grand evasion of unpleasant realities, an emotional crutch that almost begs to be pulled out from under us. Maybe it was time for these disciples to face up to the facts about Jesus and the falsehoods in their own religion.

In *The Future of an Illusion*, Freud claims that religion

functions as "a system of wishful illusions together with a disavowal of reality"—the defining feature of neurosis.[7] If, as Freud insisted, the avoidance of reality causes neurosis, then organized religion amounts to a group of neurotics who gather each Sunday for a hymn-chanting therapy session.

Best-selling authors such as Sam Harris argue exactly along these lines. In *The End of Faith*, Harris heaps abuse on religious believers for canonizing "ancient ignorance and derangement" and selling it wholesale to the masses. "And so, while religious people are not generally mad, their core beliefs absolutely are. . . . In fact, it is difficult to imagine a set of beliefs more suggestive of mental illness than those that lie at the heart of many of our religious traditions."[8]

This is not the place to debate Freudian-style skepticism. Nevertheless, we might wonder what kind of emotional personality can so easily condemn the vast majority of the world's population as a seething insane asylum. (Our psychiatric institutions, in fact, contain more than a few residents who insist that *they* are the only sane individuals in an otherwise absurd world.) If truth be told, it is not only religious believers who face the prospect of disillusionment. Secular-minded people are just as prone to the experience, the halting sense that one's bedrock beliefs have been mistaken.

Consider the fact that almost no one—no one, at least, who has ever fallen in love—escapes deep and painful disappointment in his or her relationships. Poets such as Robert Browning are notorious for idealizing the women in their lives, only to be hurled into despair when the women failed to conform to the romantic imagination. Browning admits as much in his poem "Pauline" when he writes:

And then know that this curse will come on us,
To see our idols perish; we may wither . . . [9]

Of course, poets are not the only ones to idolize romantic love. If the grim statistics about divorce are any guide, then
disenchantment with a spouse—for who gets married secretly
believing they won't be in love *forever*?—helps to destroy half of
all the marriages in the United States. "My own research speaks
to 'loss of intimacy,' in the sense that when people first become
close they feel a tremendous sense of validation from each other,
like their partner is the only other person on earth who sees
things as they do," writes Harry Reis, a social psychologist.
"That feeling sometimes fades, and when it does, it can take a
heavy toll on the marriage."[10]

The fading of our affections—what social scientists coldly
diagnose as *disillusionment*—appears to be the norm in many
marriages today. Why?

Psychologists and counselors have worried for quite some
time that the "idealization of interpersonal relationships" is
what makes marriages so unstable in the West.[11] We construct
fantasies about our partner, illusions about his or her cheerfulness, patience, empathy, sexual appeal, faith, and so on. Sooner
or later—and the sooner the better—reality intrudes into our
whitewashed relational world. Thus, counselors typically identify
disillusionment as one of the required stages of a healthy, long-
lasting marriage. Most everyone agrees that it is an inevitable
part of intimate relationships. But inevitable or not, disillusionment in romance still sends us into shock mode.

Whatever the cause, we are mesmerized by how people react
to the destruction of their dreams. The unpredictability of it

all—for no two people respond exactly the same way—can create intense drama, pathos, heroism, or despair.

No wonder it has been such a popular theme in literature. Hell hath no fury, after all, like a woman scorned. That this theme appears in some of the oldest recorded stories in Western civilization tells us something about its universality. In *The Aeneid*, for example, we read of the emotional unraveling of a woman when she learns that her lover—driven by a higher sense of duty—must abandon her forever. The embittered cry of Dido over Aeneas remains one of the most haunting laments ever recorded:

> I won't hold you, I won't even refute you—go!—
> Strike out for Italy on the winds, your realm across the sea.
> I hope, I pray, if the just gods still have any power,
> Wrecked on the rocks mid-sea you'll drink your bowl
> Of pain to the dregs, crying out the name of Dido
> Over and over, and worlds away I'll hound you then
> With pitch-black flames, and when icy death has severed
> My body from its breath, then my ghost will stalk you
> Through the world! You'll pay, you shameless, ruthless—
> And I will hear of it, yes, the report will reach me
> Even among the deepest shades of Death![12]

A crushing sense of betrayal is not confined to women, or to romantics, or to religious believers. It can strike anyone who attaches himself wholeheartedly to a great cause that ends in compromise or failure. This theme propels the fabulously popular spy story, the *Bourne* film trilogy. Jason Bourne, played by Matt Damon, is a specially trained U.S. intelligence agent suffering from amnesia and desperately trying to regain his identity.

He discovers that he has been commissioned by the CIA as an elite assassin to protect the United States from its enemies. "You said that you would do what it takes to save American lives," his CIA operative tells him in a flashback scene. "Will you give yourself to this program?"

Bourne painfully realizes that "the program" has become utterly corrupt, awash in Machiavellian ethics. Hardwired to kill, he has betrayed the ideals he set out to defend. He has murdered innocent people—collateral damage—without mercy. Bourne goes off the grid to get to the truth about his identity, while the government he swore to protect mobilizes to have him killed. As his memory slowly returns, his sense of betrayal deepens. "Everything I found out," he says, "I want to forget."

Some of the most poignant real-life examples of this experience are found among former spies for the Soviet Communist Party. In *Witness*, a classic autobiography of an ex-Communist, Whittaker Chambers describes the appeal of Marxist atheism for millions of young people around the world. Writing at the start of the Cold War, he argues that its attraction had little to do with the theatrical slogan, "Workers of the world unite! You have nothing to lose but your chains." Instead, Communism offered its followers a grandiose sense of purpose, namely, the complete transformation of modern society into a secular paradise. The belief that rallied Communists from across the frontiers of nations, across the barriers of language and class and education, was a simple conviction: it was necessary to change the world.[13]

Yet for all its talk of equality, rationality, and social justice, Communism could not conceal its wretched crimes in pursuit of its goals—the arrests, the seizure of property, the constant surveillance, the assassinations, the culture of betrayal, the concentration camps. Sooner or later, party members had to reckon in their consciences with these crimes.

Chambers relates the story of a German diplomat in Moscow, an ardent pro-Communist who became implacably anti-Communist. What brought about his conversion? Five annihilating words: *one night he heard screams.*[14]

"Those screams have reached every Communist's mind. Usually they stop there," Chambers writes. "But one day the Communist really hears those screams. He is going about his routine party tasks . . . Suddenly, there closes around that Communist a separating silence, and in that silence he hears screams. He hears them for the first time. For they do not merely reach his mind. They pierce beyond. They pierce to his soul." When Chambers allowed the screams of Communism's victims to communicate to his own soul, he abandoned the Marxist faith that had absorbed nearly his entire adult life.

Yet his rejection of Communism at first left him desolate, burdened by an enormous sense of futility and inadequacy toward his future. "The world I was returning to seemed . . . a graveyard." Only a promise to his children kept him from taking his own life.

We have to wonder whether the companions on the Emmaus road were shaken—even paralyzed—by a similar sense of desolation. They had been skeptical at first about the buzz of excitement over Jesus. But he had won them over with his words, his teaching, his mission—and his miracles.[15] For the last three years these men had uprooted their entire lives to be part of his revolution. Never had they known within themselves such courage, such a desire to take up the cause of God in the world. Never had anything in their lives seemed so important.

Up until those horrifying moments of Friday morning, when the Romans did their worst to Jesus, they would have followed him anywhere, into the darkest prison on earth. Their confession to the stranger only hints at their despair: *"We had hoped that he was the one who was going to redeem Israel."*

The War to End All Wars

Let us agree that the experience of disillusionment, whatever its cause—from misplaced political, romantic, or religious ideals—is inescapable for most of us. Joseph Priestley, an eighteenth-century minister, put it nicely: "Living in an age of advertisement, we are perpetually disillusioned. The perfect life is spread before us every day, but it changes and withers at a touch." In our own age of endless, fantastic advertisements, there is no certain refuge from the puncturing of our beliefs, for either the agnostic or the man in the pew.

Indeed, so universal and so powerful is this state of mind that it affects not only individuals, but entire cultures and societies. It is this outlook that historians most often invoke to describe the mood of the West in the years following the First World War. No conflict in modern times was initially greeted with such enthusiasm. The soldiers of the armies of Europe, many of them hungry for the glory of combat, marched out of their capitals in the weeks of August 1914 before rapturous crowds. Women showered them with flowers. Bands played patriotic hymns. Old men wept with joy and longing, anticipating the return of national greatness. "If you were a young man," recalled an Australian veteran, "it was the thing to do."[16]

In the previous century, Europeans had been spared the ravages of a protracted, wide-ranging war. Many had come to glamorize military conquest. Most of the participants imagined that the war would solve their economic and political problems. German strategists such as Carl von Clausewitz helped persuade military leaders that wars could be politically useful, economical—and short. Everyone expected that the Great War, as it came to be called, would be over by Christmas. The German Kaiser spoke for many when he told departing troops in the first week of August: "You will be home before the leaves have fallen from the trees."[17]

It was a pleasant illusion.

There were no decisive victories in the early days of battle. Soldiers settled into a defensive posture, building a series of trenches that stretched from northern France to the Swiss border. The new industrialized approach to warfare—machine guns, howitzers, battleships, submarines, tanks, barbed wire, poison gas—helped ensure that the conflict would be long, desperate, and heartless.

No one could have imagined the result: a four-year conflict whose death toll exceeded that of all other wars known in human history. At least ten million men perished, or about 5,600 soldiers killed every day for the length of the war. Many wondered what, if anything, the conflict accomplished. As Winston Churchill summarized it, "The whole life energy of the greatest nations had been poured out in wrath and slaughter."[18]

It is hard to overstate the horror and nearly pathological gloom in the aftermath of the war. For more than a century before the First World War, the West—including its secular elites—imagined itself on a happy, upward trajectory. There were, to be sure, great strides in technology, medicine, and scientific knowledge. The Industrial Revolution was lifting millions of Europeans out of poverty. Nation-states were becoming more egalitarian and democratic. The watchword was *progress*—political, technological, economic, moral, and spiritual. Thus, in the minds of many, including many Christian ministers, the war would further the ideals of democracy and Christianity. Baptist leader James Francis, upon America's entry into the conflict, declared thus: "I look upon the enlistment of an American soldier as I do on the departure of a missionary for Burma."[19]

The Great War demolished all of these notions. In her Pulitzer prize–winning book *The Guns of August*, Barbara Tuchman explains the psychological effect of the conflict:

> Men could not sustain a war of such magnitude and pain without hope—the hope that its very enormity would ensure that it could never happen again and the hope that when somehow it had been fought through to a resolution, the foundations of a better-ordered world would have been laid . . . . Nothing less could give dignity or sense to the monstrous offensives in which thousands and hundreds of thousands were killed to gain ten yards and exchange one wet-bottomed trench for another. When every autumn people said it could not last through the winter, and when every spring there was still no end in sight, only the hope that out of it all some good would accrue to mankind kept men and nations fighting. When at last it was over, the war had many diverse results, and one dominant one transcending all others: disillusion.[20]

Anyone who clung to the belief that European culture had advanced the cause of humanity need only visit the battlefields of Flanders, the monuments to the dead at Verdun, the cemeteries scattered across Europe. "We have lost all feeling for one another," admits Eric Maria Remarque in *All Quiet on the Western Front.* "We are insensible, dead men, who through some trick, some dreadful magic, are still able to run and kill."[21] The most advanced, rational, and civilized nations of the earth had failed to prevent the worst conflict in human history. The verdict was in: progress was an illusion.

The Betrayal of a Great Faith

Even as the West was enduring the disintegration of its dreams of progress, the world of Islam was undergoing its own form of disillusionment. For centuries after their first appearance in the sands of Arabia, Muslims viewed themselves as the vanguard of a new civilization—a community of believers commissioned by Allah to spread the faith of Muhammad, their great prophet, throughout the world. For a time, Islam claimed the most powerful military force on earth. It was the leading economic power, with trading posts in Asia, Europe, and Africa. Islamic arts and sciences rivaled or surpassed anything achieved in Europe. The future, it seemed, belong to Islam.

But not for long. Internal divisions and military defeats helped put Islam on a course of decline. "The fleet of the divinely guided Empire encountered the fleet of the wretched infidels," wrote a commanding officer at the battle of Lepanto in 1571, "and the will of Allah turned the other way."[22] The "infidel" Europeans continued to make scientific and technological breakthroughs that left the cultural heritage of Islam far behind.

The *coup de grâce* was the dreary fate of the Ottoman

Empire—"the sick man of Europe"—at the end of the First World War. The Turkish Empire represented the last great stronghold of Islam. It was led by a caliph, a religious ruler who embodied the political and spiritual authority for all of Islam. Like the old Holy Roman Emperors, he had no rivals in his kingdom. It was his duty to protect the Islamic community, to lead Muslims into battle, and to implement Islamic law, or *sharia*. As "Commander of the Faithful," the caliph was the last in the line of rulers who dated back to the death of the prophet Muhammad in AD 632. Even in its weakened condition, the existence of the caliphate held out the hope of a reinvigorated Islam.

Those hopes exploded after the First World War, with Turkey's military defeat and political disintegration. Even before the outbreak of the war, the empire was melting like a spring snow. Writes historian Margaret MacMillan: "The power of the throne, which had once made the world tremble, had slipped away."[23] The final remnants of the Ottoman Empire were divided up as French and British mandates after the war. All Islamic lands, except Turkey, were placed under European rule.[24]

The greatest indignity arrived when Turkey's new leader, Mustafa Kemal Atatürk, announced his plan to "modernize" his nation along Western lines. He imposed a secular regime on Turkey's Muslim population. On March 3, 1924, he abolished the Ottoman Caliphate. Atatürk's action was seen as a great betrayal of Islam; zealous believers called it "the mother of all crimes." In a videotaped message a few weeks after the 9/11 attacks, Osama bin Laden complained about the humiliation and disgrace suffered by Islam for more than eighty years—meaning the destruction of the Ottoman Caliphate at the hands of Western infidels.

Muslims all over the world became embittered by the collapse of their spiritual leadership. "The primacy and therefore the dominance of the West was clear for all to see," writes Bernard Lewis, "invading every aspect of the Muslim's public and even—more painfully—his private life."[25] Many began asking: How could the civilization of Islam become so debased and subjugated at the hands of infidels? What went wrong?

The Hope of Israel

We may suspect that the two travelers on the road to Emmaus felt something like this, the repudiation of their most cherished assumptions about the future. For it is the experience of disillusionment, above all others, that sets these men to flight. Notice again their candid confession about Jesus recorded for us in Luke's gospel: *"We had hoped that he was the one who was going to redeem Israel."* The "redemption" or restoration of Israel as a political and religious community was a theme that had fired the imagination of Jews for centuries.

Think about the remarkable history of the Jewish people, as passed down from generation to generation. Through their great patriarch, Abraham, they were brought into a special relationship, or covenant, with God. They were promised a physical and spiritual inheritance: the land of Canaan, as well as the presence of God himself in their midst. They escaped the bondage of Egypt, endured a long desert exodus, and took possession of the land God had promised them. Slaves and the children of slaves became victorious warriors and landowners. God had shown the Jews—and the world—that he could deliver his people from the greatest empire on earth.

This resilient and proud nation, however, watched in horror the destruction of their temple in Jerusalem and the devastating defeats by the Assyrian and Babylonian armies. Most Jews had been either killed in battle or dragged off as prisoners of war. A remnant of their nation survived and managed to rebuild their holy temple. But the Jews remained under foreign domination, second-class citizens wherever they lived.

Israel's greatest prophets all gave voice to the trauma of a people in crisis. As biblical scholar John Goldingay describes it, the nation was handed over—like a condemned criminal—to servitude, exile, plunder, dishonor, and death. She was taunted, broken, forgotten, cast off, and powerless, like a bird at the mercy of predators. Jerusalem was no longer the sanctuary of God. Instead, the holy city was a lonely widow, weeping, betrayed, homeless, distressed, and disillusioned.[26] "Bitterly she weeps at night, tears are on her cheeks. . . . All her gateways are desolate, her priests groan, her young women grieve, and she is in bitter anguish."[27] The God of Abraham seemed to have utterly abandoned his people.

Yet, amid all the lamentations, there is a message of hope—the hope of rescue and restoration.

The disciples on the Emmaus road had read the prophets of Israel and believed them when they promised that the nation would not grieve forever. The Jews would not disappear from the face of the earth, nor remain despised among the nations. God himself would act on their behalf.

The prophet Isaiah boldly proclaimed divine judgment against Israel's enemies and restoration for the Jewish people: "The LORD will have compassion on Jacob; once again he will choose Israel and will settle them in their own land. . . . They will make captives of their captors and rule over their oppressors."[28] Jeremiah acknowledged Israel's disobedience to God, but he held out a promise of forgiveness, rescue, and renewal. "Because of your great guilt and many sins I have done these things to you. But all who devour you will be devoured; all your enemies will go into exile. . . . I will restore you to health and heal your wounds."[29]

To the Jewish people, the promise was certain. The political and spiritual restoration of Israel would arrive, but only after another prophet, a man sent by God—a *Messiah*—led the way forward.

The hope of a Messiah loomed large in the life of every Jew in Palestine. As the prophets described him, he would be a king, descended from King David himself—only far greater in strength and influence. From the prophet Nathan came this promise to David and to Israel: "I will raise up your offspring to succeed you . . . and I will establish the throne of his kingdom forever."[30] Zechariah spoke of him this way: "See, your king comes to you, righteous and having salvation . . . His rule will extend from sea to sea and from the River to the ends of the earth."[31] Isaiah's description would stir the hearts of Jews for generations: "For to us a child is born, to us a son is given. . . . And he will be called Wonderful Counselor, Mighty God, Everlasting Father, Prince of Peace. Of the greatness of his government and peace there will be no end. He will reign on David's throne and over his kingdom, establishing and upholding it with justice and righteousness from that time on and forever."[32]

To the Jews in Jesus' day, the anticipated king and Messiah would be an awesome figure indeed—empowered by God to crush the hated Romans, destroy the enemies of Israel, gather the faithful together, and establish political and religious sovereignty over all the nations of the earth.[33] As any believing Jew would tell you, the "kingdom of heaven" meant the kingdom of Israel, gloriously restored and governed by God through the Messiah.

The two friends on the Emmaus road had cherished these promises from Scripture all their lives. But the prophets had declared their messages of hope a long, long time ago—hundreds of years before they were born—to no effect. Israel remained under the boot of a pagan empire. As one generation after another came and went, the voice of God remained mute. As far as anyone could tell, there was not a single prophet among the Jews, and no prospect of one showing up anytime soon.

And then the Teacher from Nazareth appeared. Jesus certainly sounded like a prophet of old: a man in complete possession of himself and his message. He spoke with fearless authority, as if to ignore him was to taunt heaven itself. He worked miracles not heard of since the days of Ezekiel. He not only understood Israel's history, he described its history as though he himself were the hand guiding it. "Jerusalem, Jerusalem," he said, "you who kill the prophets and stone those sent to you, how often I have longed to gather your children together, as a hen gathers her chicks under her wings, and you were not willing."[34] Through the life and teaching of Jesus, God's promise to the Jewish people was finally being realized: the Messiah, the Great Rescuer, seemed to have arrived.

All of this is what made the death of Jesus so devastating. Other leaders in Israel had suffered at the hands of pagan rulers. Isaiah himself died a martyr for his message. But Jesus was not supposed to follow this unhappy script in Israel's history; he was to be the last prophet, the last messenger sent from heaven to finally and fully restore Israel. Now it all looked like a wretched mistake. After everything was said and done, he was the wrong man.

There was no escaping the truth of it. The final prophet in God's long history of prophets—the Messiah—could not possibly be defeated by God's enemies.

The problem for these two travelers to Emmaus is not simply that they were wrong about Jesus. They were wrong about *everything*. They were wrong about his miracles, wrong about the truth of his teaching, wrong to think that God was at work again on Israel's behalf. *"We had hoped that he was the one who was going to redeem Israel."* All of their hopes—all the promises of rescue and triumph over their enemies—had come to nothing.

What, now, are they to do? It is this question that surely haunts and harasses these men as they make their way home.

When Faith Falters

Perhaps it is the same question that faces many of us now: What are we to do? After what has just happened in our lives—the failure, the betrayal, the suffering, the death—what are we supposed to do? What are we supposed to believe?

All of us who have experienced great disillusionment in life know that it serves at least one worthy purpose: it helps us to see the world as it actually is, not as we would like it to be. No one grows in wisdom by willfully clinging to falsehoods about life. It is a humbling experience to admit we have been wrong about big things, about questions that really matter. Yet a little humility is often just what we need to prod us forward in search of better answers.

Singers and songwriters are often reaching toward this idea. Country music legend Johnny Cash seemed to personify the disillusioned man: jaded by the brutal realities of life, yet determined to somehow carry on.

When Cash died in 2003, he was lauded by the *New York Times* for his ability to "erase the lines between singing, storytelling and grueling life experience." The plaintive "Hurt," for example, recorded near the end of his life, is thick with the pain of bad choices and broken promises. In the end, the singer renounces his "empire of dirt." Like few other artists, Cash identified with the cynics and sinners among us. As the *New York Times* put it: "The sinners that Johnny Cash sang about, unlike those in most gangsta rap songs, were usually plagued by guilt and in search of God's forgiveness."[35]

Religious leaders could learn a thing or two from "the man in black." Smug in their theological certainties, they often forget that no matter where we are on the road to Emmaus, we all nurture illusions about God. Fortunately, he has no illusions about us. If the Christian story describes the world as it actually is, then God is intimately aware of all our struggles, our sins, our tragedies, our sorrows. He is closer to us than we are to ourselves. If this is so, then there can be no real consolation, no deep confidence about the meaning of our lives—no end to our disillusionment—until we come to know the love of God for us.

Many are ready to abandon the search for God and truth because they have been deceived. The people or ideas they once trusted in have failed them in some way, and they've had enough. Others consider themselves honest agnostics about spiritual issues. They've seen the damage done by those armed with absolute answers to just about every question, and they want no part of it. They want to see a little more modesty among the true believers.

I confess that I'm pretty sympathetic to the doubters among us. The reputation of Christians today is a little like that of British prime minister Clement Attlee, expressed by the indomitable Winston Churchill. "Mr. Attlee is a very modest man," Churchill said. "But then he has much to be modest about."[36]

A little more humility in matters of faith would be a good thing for most of us. Is it a sign of modesty, though, to presume that nothing—absolutely nothing—can be known about God with any confidence? Great thinkers such as Pascal didn't believe so. A crisis of faith sent Pascal reeling down his own Emmaus road. And yet he considered it "an indispensable obligation" for people to keep seeking the truth about God in the teeth of their darkest doubts. "There are only two classes of persons who can be called reasonable," he wrote. "Those who serve God with all their heart because they know him and those who seek him with all their heart because they do not know him."[37]

The two friends on the road to Emmaus have begun to realize that some of their most deeply held beliefs have been miserably mistaken. Yet despite their pain and disillusionment, they have not given up their quest to know God. In fact, they are on the knife's edge of the greatest discovery of their lives.

5

RUMORS OF ANGELS

"Some of our women amazed us. They went
to the tomb early this morning but didn't
find his body. They came and told us that
they had seen a vision of angels, who said he
was alive."

Life *magazine called it "the Bronx Miracle." On November 14, 1945,
just after the end of the Second World War, nearly thirty thousand
people crowded into a lot in a New York City neighborhood, outside
the home of nine-year-old Joseph Vitolo. Two weeks earlier, Vitolo had
told his playground friends that the Virgin Mary appeared to him in
a vision—and that she would reappear each day for sixteen days, after
which "something wonderful would happen."*

*For the next two weeks, pilgrims made their way to a makeshift
shrine at the intersection of the Grand Concourse and Van Cortlandt
Avenue in the Bronx. Each night, after finishing dinner with his Italian
family, Vitolo knelt at the spot of the first appearance. Each night, he
said, the virgin appeared to him as he prayed. Many found him credible,*

and a steady stream of onlookers soon became a flood. Mothers who had lost sons in the war came for comfort. Wounded soldiers sought healing. Priests took confession and offered benedictions. Even Hollywood celebrities, including Frank Sinatra, reportedly paid a visit.

Eventually they came by the thousands, arriving by foot, cars, and buses, to catch a glimpse of the apparition. They brought candles and rosaries, recited prayers, and sang hymns. Some claimed a miraculous healing; others fainted from shock. By the last night of the vigil, news of the sightings had spread around the country. People were arriving from Philadelphia, Jersey City, and even Canada. They gathered in a steady, cold rain, under a tapestry of umbrellas, to hear a message from heaven.

What was the message?

The Blessed Mother apparently didn't have much to say. She asked Joseph to pray for peace on earth. She asked him if he knew about Bernadette. She gave Joseph a medal with healing powers, which apparently got lost in the confusion. After a couple of hours, people began to peel away from the scene. Other than a break in the rain after Joseph finished praying, there was no agreement that anything out of the ordinary had happened.[1]

———◦◦———

Back in the 1990s, books about angels and other supernatural visitors began to invade bookstores like cicadas in summertime. Self-proclaimed experts in angel activity hit the lecture and talk-show circuit. Newsmagazines ran cover stories exploring the explosion of interest. In 1993, five of the ten best-selling paperbacks were about angels. ABC aired a two-hour prime time special, *Angels: The Mysterious Messengers*. A *Time* magazine poll found that a third of all adults claimed to have felt an angelic presence at some point in their lives. "Angels are appearing everywhere in America," proclaimed *Newsweek*. "Having trouble recognizing the angels among us? Join an angel focus group."[2]

The interest in heavenly beings seems insatiable. Beliefnet. com has an ongoing feature, "Explore Our Angels Community." The bimonthly magazine *Angels on Earth*, which highlights stories of people who believe they have encountered angels, boasts more than a million readers. There are scores of angel boutique shops, seminars, and websites. Amazon lists nearly 2,500 books on the subject, including *Angels in My Hair* and *The Angel Therapy Handbook*. Whether they involve winged creatures in the clouds, smiling women in white, cherubic crystals, weeping statues, the appearance of the stigmata—these and other phenomena are offered up as evidence of spiritual activity in our lives. God is supposedly grabbing our attention through these potent signs of the paranormal.

But this ought to make any thinking person wonder: For the love of God, what exactly is he trying to tell us?

Unlike most alleged sightings of the supernatural, Luke's reference to the women at the tomb of Jesus is notable for its clarity. The angels they encounter have news about Jesus, and there is nothing enigmatic about the message: *"They came and told us that they had seen a vision of angels, who said he was alive."* We'll explore the content of this angelic announcement in a moment. For now it is enough to say that the message is concise and concrete: Jesus, who was crucified, has risen from the dead. There are no blathering generalities about divine love or prayers for peace in our time. Other than the angels, neither are there any strange phenomena at the scene—no holy grail, no bleeding rocks, no magical medallions. There are just the grave-clothes of Jesus and an empty tomb.

Parking-Space Angels

As we noted in chapter 1, the modern, scientific mind has trouble with stories that reach beyond the explainable, natural world. Tales of angels are even tougher to swallow because, in our own day at least, they seem tailor made to meet our emotional needs. If they didn't exist, we'd have to invent them.

Take, for example, *Angels 101: An Introduction to Connecting, Working, and Healing with the Angels*, written by metaphysician Doreen Virtue. We are informed that, in contrast to the ideas of sin and guilt in some religious traditions, angels love every person unconditionally. They help everyone who calls on them, regardless of their religious faith or lack of it. "They look past the surface and see the godliness within all of us," she writes. "So angels aren't judgmental, and they only bring love into our lives. You're safe with the angels, and you can totally trust them."[3]

Angels, according to Virtue, not only are accepting of us, warts and all, but are also eager to help us fulfill our dreams of happiness. In fact, there is nothing more important to our angels than helping us, and there is no need too small or insignificant to merit their assistance. A frequent conference speaker worldwide, Virtue lists the many ways that angels can be counted on to assist people, even in mapping out their travel plans. They will:

- Help you get an extremely nice, warm, friendly, and competent customer-service representative when calling an airline to book reservations
- Help you avoid lines at check-in, and work with sweet and competent personnel
- Let you sail through airport security without being searched
- Protect and deliver your baggage so that your suitcases are the first ones on the luggage carousel when you're there to collect it[4]

You get the idea. With angels on your side, you can travel as if you were a member of Hollywood's glitterati, untouched by the petty inconveniences that afflict the sweaty masses. You can even sashay through airports without worrying about being manhandled by security personnel. Like bellhops at the Ritz-Carlton, these spiritual servants are at your beck and call, round the clock. They make no demands on us; rather, they wait to be summoned to help us overcome every difficulty: "You never have to be afraid that the angels would ever ask you to do anything that would make you feel afraid."[5]

With her appearances on CNN, *Oprah*, and *The View*, Virtue's message—shared by many other authors in the field—clearly has a large audience. "I've discovered that the quickest and most efficient route to happiness is through connecting with the angels," she writes. "So whether you need help with your health, career, love life, family, or any other area, the angels can help you."[6] Yes, even your sex life can be improved with a little angelic assistance, whatever that might mean.

Think about the angels that have populated Hollywood movies over the years. There was the lovable but bumbling Clarence in *It's a Wonderful Life* (1946), and the charming and sophisticated Dudley, played by Cary Grant, in *The Bishop's Wife* (1947). More recently, in films such as *Michael* (1996), John Travolta played—what else?—a dancing angel.

In *City of Angels* (1998), an angel named Seth (Nicolas Cage) falls in love with an earth-bound nurse, Maggie (Meg Ryan). Seth abandons his angelic status for a relationship with Maggie, only to watch her die in a bike accident. Asked if he regrets his decision to become human, he answers: "I would rather have had one breath of her hair, one kiss of her mouth, one touch of her hand, than eternity without it." In other words, the secret of a happy life is found on planet earth, not in the heavens with God.

In *Legion* (2009), the pro-humanity message is taken as far as it can go, even as angels take on a much darker persona. In this gory thriller, the archangel Michael descends to earth to defend mankind against . . . God himself. Why? God has lost faith in human beings and decided to unleash a legion of angels, led by Gabriel, to destroy them.

The final confrontation reflects either Hollywood's limited imagination or limited budget, as a greasy diner in the California desert becomes the scene of humanity's last bold stand for survival. A bizarre mix of biblical apocalypse and zombie horror, the film was widely panned, including this review: "I got an angel with a machine gun in a war determining the fate of mankind that . . . should have been over in a matter of seconds, but somehow managed to last an hour and 40 minutes."[7] Nevertheless, the film grossed $60 million.

Angels for Grown-Ups

The angels mentioned at the tomb of Jesus, however, are neither romancers nor rebels. They are not in the wish-granting business. Instead, they are portrayed as fearsome messengers obedient only to God, like other angels described throughout the Scriptures.

In fact, there are more than three hundred references to angels in the Bible, from Genesis to Revelation, and there is an impressive consistency to these accounts. While contemporary stories about angel encounters describe them as soothing and reassuring, most every reference in the Bible portrays them as confrontational: they have either a message to deliver or a task to perform. Sometimes the message is celebratory, as in the announcement of the birth of Jesus: "I bring you good news of great joy that will be for all the people."[8] But more often it involves a frightful warning, a command to change course, or a summons to obey the divine will.

In the days of Abraham, on the plain west of the Dead Sea, two angels burst out of the city gate of Sodom. With them were a man named Lot, his wife, and their two daughters. As we read in Genesis, the city had become so violent and corrupt that God sent these angels to destroy it. Thanks to the intervention of Abraham, Lot and his family were to be spared, but only if they left everything and got out of the city. "Flee for your lives!" one of the creatures commanded them. "Don't look back, and don't stop anywhere in the plain! Flee to the mountains or you will be swept away."[9]

Much later in Jewish history, an "angel of the Lord" was sent to defend Judah, the southern kingdom of Israel, against an attack by the massive and marauding Assyrian army. On the night before the invasion, we are told, an angel swept through the Assyrian camp and put to death 185,000 men. One of Lord Byron's best-known poems, "The Destruction of Sennacherib," describes the event:

> The Assyrian came down like the wolf on the fold,
> And his cohorts were gleaming in purple and gold;
> And the sheen of their spears was like stars on the sea,
> When the blue wave rolls nightly on deep Galilee. . . .
> For the Angel of Death spread his wings on the blast,
> And breathed in the face of the foe as he pass'd;
> And the eyes of the sleepers wax'd deadly and chill,
> And their hearts but once heaved, and for ever grew still![10]

Put simply, some of the most famous angel stories in Western literature depict them as dreadful harbingers of divine judgment. You won't find this kind of creature in *The Angel Therapy Handbook*.

Yet if these spiritual beings do exist, and function as God's servants and ambassadors on earth, then we should not expect them to cater to our whims or nurture our self-esteem. Rather, we should expect them to say and do things that trouble us, shock us, or make us afraid. For to find oneself in the company of an angel is to be in the presence of a spiritual being in close communion with a holy God—an intimacy no human being can now enjoy. "God made man a little lower than the angels," quipped Will Rogers, "and he has been getting a little lower ever since."

The skeptical mind, of course, will probably never accept the idea of angels. But let us at least admit that the Christian view of these messengers is not the stuff of childhood daydreams or spiritual therapists. Unlike the contemporary varieties, the angels in Scripture are always one-way messengers—they deliver

God's communication to us, not the other way around. No one ever tells an angel what to do or sends him on a shopping errand. When an angel in the Bible makes himself known, the people around him simply listen, usually with their heads bowed, and always with a sense of awe or even dread.

This is exactly the kind of encounter that the women experienced at the tomb of Jesus. In Matthew's rendering, we learn that the angels appeared to Roman guards, who were posted at the tomb to ward off potential thieves. "The guards were so afraid of him," Matthew writes, "that they shook and became like dead men."[11] Luke tells us that when the angels came and stood beside the women, they "bowed down with their faces to the ground" in a state of fear and shock.[12]

In popular imagination, angels act "like a castle moat, protecting you from negativity."[13] The angels in our story, however, act like soldiers on a life-or-death mission, who offer no guarantees of personal comfort or safety.

How to Get God on Your Side

Regardless how angels are described, many will object that for centuries religious people have used angels to rationalize their pet projects. What better way to vindicate your agenda than by the appearance of an angel or other heavenly sign?

These critics have a point. Sometimes angelic sightings have been used as evidence of divine displeasure, a way of explaining devastating plagues or earthquakes—and condemning sinners and other enemies of the church. In Islam, it was an angel sent by God who reportedly revealed the entire text of the Qur'an to Muhammad, giving it an unassailable moral authority. After all, angels don't lie. In Judaism, as we have seen, angels are sometimes described as agents of death among God's foes. In the history of Christianity, some of the most troubling episodes involve church authorities legitimizing military campaigns with supernatural signs. A messenger from heaven supposedly commanded the victory—a holy war.

One of the most notorious examples of this occurred in the early fourth century AD. Church historians tell us that at about noontime, October 27, 312, a Roman commander was readying his troops for battle. For six years he had been fighting against various contenders to rule the empire, following the resignation of the latest emperor, Diocletian. Now this commander was preparing to square off against his archrival, Maxentius, who controlled Rome. Forces were massing at a bridge just outside the city. Suddenly the commander saw a sign from heaven: a cross of light in the skies, accompanied by an inscription, *Conquer by this*. In a dream later that night, it was explained to him that he should inscribe "the heavenly sign of God" on his soldiers' shields "as a safeguard in all engagements with his enemies."[14]

The commander awoke at dawn, told the miracle to his friends, and was obedient to the vision. He fashioned his army's standard with the letters "chi-rho" (the first two Greek letters in the name of *Christ*) and fixed them to his helmet. He met the army of Maxentius that day at the Battle of the Milvian Bridge, just north of Rome by the Tiber River. His opponent was forced back toward the river. The bridge was too narrow to support their retreat, and their overloaded boats sank in the Tiber, drowning hundreds. Among them was Maxentius, pulled down into the mud of the riverbed by the weight of his armor.

Although significantly outnumbered, the commander's forces were victorious. The next day the general strode triumphant through the gates of Rome at the front of his army. He claimed later, as noted in a Latin inscription under his statue in Rome:

> By this savior sign, the truest test of bravery, I saved and freed
> your city from the yoke of the tyrant, and restored the Senate
> and the Roman people, freed, to their ancient fame and splendor.

It was an astonishing turnaround. A Roman general in a pagan empire—defending a violent regime hostile to Christianity since its inception—marched into the capital under the sign of the cross. The general's name, of course, was Constantine. Thanks to his heavenly vision, Rome exchanged the protective embrace of its gods and goddesses for the arms of Jesus Christ.

Often forgotten is what Constantine did immediately after settling into the imperial palace as the new ruler. Rome's first "Christian emperor," the man who paved the way for the conversion of the empire to Christianity, ordered the execution of the "nearest friends" of his predecessor. Not known for his subtlety, Constantine put the head of his military opponent, Maxentius, in a box and had it shipped to his enemies in North Africa. The message: there is a new ruler in Rome, and you'd better line up to pay him homage.

Angels in a Graveyard

So we must be honest about the use and abuse of angels and other heavenly signs to support an earthly agenda. But that fact doesn't tell us anything about these creatures, or what role they might actually play in the Christian story. Why, we might ask, are there angels mentioned at all in the gospel accounts? If Jesus has risen from the dead, can't he simply announce that news all by himself?

These are questions for theologians, but as a layman, let me offer a theory that seems consistent with what we have already noticed in the Emmaus story. We have seen how a stranger, allegedly Jesus himself, comes alongside the two disciples, who are *"kept from recognizing him."* The implication is that they are not emotionally prepared to meet Jesus alive again after the experience of his execution. They need time to grasp the inconceivable truth of the thing—that somehow he has overcome death itself.

It seems likely that the women at the tomb of Jesus are in a similar state of mind. All of them, we are told, witnessed first-hand his horrifying martyrdom. They literally watched him breathe his last breath. These women are not at the tomb to enjoy morning tea with Jesus; they have come to prepare his body for its final burial. But things are not as they should be: *"Some of our women amazed us. They went to the tomb early this morning but didn't find his body."* What they find is an empty grave—the large stone that had covered it has been rolled away—and they are completely disoriented by their discovery.

We must not forget, as the gospels make a point of reminding us, that these women are real people, with real personalities and attachments, each with a unique relationship to Jesus before his death. When most of the male disciples are keeping a low profile behind closed doors, it is these women who rise at dawn and leave their homes to offer a final act of service to their crucified leader. It is these women, as one author put it, who "bore the whole brunt of the crisis" that had descended on the Jesus movement after his death.[15]

Who are these valiant and resolute women? One of them is Mary, the mother of James, one of the dozen men handpicked to live in close, everyday friendship with Jesus as his disciples. Like her son, she seems to have been a devoted follower of Jesus since the start of his ministry. As the mother of a member of this inner ring of disciples, Mary would have known Jesus more intimately than the vast majority of his followers.

Another of the women named is Joanna, identified earlier in Luke's story as the wife of a powerful official employed by Herod Antipas—the same ruler of Galilee who had a hand in the trial and execution of Jesus. We're told that Joanna was among the many women who helped support the ministry of Jesus and the apostles, which is plausible given that her husband, a man called Chuza, served as Herod's chief financial officer. Joanna is not only a woman of means, but also a risk-taker who put her family's wealth at the disposal of a person opposed by most of the religious establishment.

A third woman in the story is Mary from Magdala, a tiny fishing village along the Sea of Galilee. Luke tells us that Jesus brought remarkable spiritual healing to Mary, rescuing her from demons that had complete control over her life. A profound change must have occurred because her commitment to Jesus is unshakeable. She leaves her home in Galilee to support his ministry, wherever it takes her. She is the first person mentioned among the group of women who venture to the dreadful scene of his crucifixion. She is the last person to leave the gravesite. "Then the disciples went back to where they were staying," writes the apostle John, but "Mary stood outside the tomb crying."[16]

Thus the question remains: Why are there angels at the burial site of Jesus, announcing his resurrection to these women?

Let us consider again what must have been their mental outlook as they approached the tomb. In the Jewish faith at this time, the most important obligation of friends and family members to the deceased is to make sure the body is prepared properly for burial. According to custom, an anointing should be completed before the body begins to decompose, reckoned within three days. This was considered the responsibility of women. Thus, after observing the Sabbath on Saturday, the women buy spices and go to the tomb at the first possible opportunity, early Sunday morning.

Each of these women were devoted to Jesus—so devoted that they made significant sacrifices, and took great personal risks, to support his ministry and honor him in his death. "What urged these women to hazard life and body?" asked Martin Luther. "It was nothing but the great love they bore to the Lord, which had sunk so deeply into their hearts that for his sake they would have risked a thousand lives."[17]

Nonetheless, they have no reason in the world to hope that Jesus might be alive; their Jewish faith offered them none. "For most Jews . . . the grave marked the final end of a man's story. Death was seen as inescapable and universal," writes the renowned Jewish scholar Geza Vermes. "For the down-to-earth Jew of the biblical era, death was simply the common heritage of all the living."[18] Later we'll explore in more depth the beliefs of the ancient world about death and what might lie beyond it. For now, it is enough to say this: although Jews believed that a person's spirit might live on, his body was forever consigned to the dustbin of the earth.

So a group of women descend upon a graveyard in the

half-light of early dawn. These women—individuals with deep personal attachments to Jesus—are the first to arrive at the scene. They are shaken by grief and filled with anxiety about the future. They would have been overwhelmed by the sudden appearance of the Teacher. Who wouldn't be? They need to be prepared in some way, both intellectually and emotionally, for his resurrection. The angels provide this preparation: *"They came and told us that they had seen a vision of angels, who said he was alive."* The angels, who have taken the form of men dressed in white, can deliver the astonishing news so that it might be understood and received.

Finding God in *The Lord of the Rings*

In a 1947 review of *The Bishop's Wife*, a film critic for the *New York Times* dismissed the idea of angelic visitations as "sentimental whimsy" and expressed the view typical of our sophisticated age: "All of us know that angels don't walk the earth like natural men."[19]

Often there is a massive gulf between what we say we know and what we actually believe. For whatever we finally believe about angels and their role in our lives, we can't seem to shake ourselves loose from the idea of them, even as our society becomes more openly secular. It is not the cotton candy, therapeutic angels I now have in mind. I mean instead those versions that come closest to the biblical depictions of angels—with their authoritative presence, martial strength, and unwavering obedience to a transcendent cause.

There is no greater portrait of an angelic figure in modern fiction or film than the character sketched in J. R. R. Tolkien's

The Lord of the Rings. Tolkien readers will know exactly whom I mean: Gandalf the Grey.

For those not familiar with the story, *The Lord of the Rings* trilogy is about an epic struggle between the noble inhabitants of a mythic world, called Middle-earth, and the Dark Lord of Mordor, the embodiment of evil bent on totalitarian rule and the annihilation of all who resist. The center of their attention is a powerful and mysterious Ring, created by the Dark Lord to give him control over Middle-earth, but now in the possession of a humble Hobbit of the Shire, Frodo Baggins. Led by Gandalf the Grey, one of the last of the great Wizards, Frodo and his allies must journey to the Cracks of Doom in the Fire-mountain to destroy the Ring and finally defeat the Dark Lord.

Like biblical angels, the Wizards are commanded to help the inhabitants of Middle-earth—men, Hobbits, Elves, and Dwarves—by their counsel and persuasion. They are immensely powerful beings, but they never use their power for their own purposes; they wield it only to combat the wicked forces of Mordor and to defend Middle-earth and its allies. As Gandalf reassures Frodo, "there has never been a day when the Shire has not been guarded by watchful eyes."[20]

Gandalf also displays a moral stature that suggests the holiness of Old Testament prophets. He understands with perfect clarity the demonic and irresistible influence of the Ring, with its capacity to intoxicate and corrupt its owner with promises of power. Determined to avoid its temptations, Gandalf will not allow himself to possess it. "A mortal, Frodo, who keeps one of the Great Rings, does not die, but he does not grow or obtain more life, he merely continues, until at last every minute is a weariness," he warns. "Yes, sooner or later—later, if he is strong or well-meaning to begin with, but neither strength nor good purpose will last—sooner or later the dark power will devour him."[21]

Although unflinchingly opposed to evil, Gandalf demonstrates a heart of compassion that approaches the divine. Throughout the story, Frodo and the "Fellowship of the Ring" are dogged by Gollum, a violent and despicable creature whose tortured soul was poisoned by his own misuse of the Ring. More than once Frodo yearns to see him killed, even as Gandalf counsels mercy:

> "I can't understand you," Frodo complains. "He deserves death."
>
> "Deserves it! I daresay he does," replies Gandalf. "Many that live deserve death. And some that die deserve life. Can you give it to them? Then do not be too eager to deal out death in judgment. For even the very wise cannot see all ends. I have not much hope that Gollum can be cured before he dies, but there is a chance of it."[22]

Despite his magical powers, there is no hint of pride in this great wizard. Rather, Gandalf possesses a magnificent self-forgetfulness. He instantly takes up any burden in service to his mission, a cause given to him from a source of goodness above and beyond him. Always mindful of those he is charged to protect, he nonetheless challenges them—Frodo most of all—to face all dangers and prove themselves faithful to their great calling. In his correspondence, Tolkien himself refers to Gandalf as an "angel incarnate."

If this is what Tolkien had in mind, then he has created one of the most compelling angels in modern literature. Literary critic Mary Hoffman has called Gandalf "the best white wizard in fiction."[23] Although *Lord of the Rings* succeeds as a masterpiece of

fantasy at several levels—its sheer imaginative force, its emphasis on sacrifice and friendship—the story is driven forward by
Gandalf's personality, even when he is not present in the scenes
described. Several years ago, Britain's Waterstones bookstores
and Channel 4 TV asked readers to vote for the greatest book of
the twentieth century. Tolkien's epic topped the list.[24]

This angelic figure, Gandalf, is a rebuke to religious believers and to skeptics alike. On the one hand, many people of faith
have turned angels into mealy-mouthed muppets—reliably
docile and endlessly pliable. They inspire neither fear nor admi-
ration. On the other hand, skeptics claim to abhor the very idea
of heavenly beings. In reality, however, they quietly admire the
angelic Gandalf as much as any Hobbit in the Shire. What many
doubters dismiss, and what many believers debase, is something
very close to the character of God himself.

As a Christian believer, Tolkien was clearly shaped by his
understanding of the divine. Giving this vision expression, in the
character of Gandalf, seems to have been part of his conscious
design. "The chief purpose of life for any of us," he said, "is to
increase according to our capacity our knowledge of God by all
means we have, and to be moved by it to praise and thanks."[25]

The Silent Witness

Some will wonder if belief in angels is really necessary in order
to draw near toward God. A better question is, what do we make
of the announcement from the angels at the tomb of Jesus? For
it is precisely this message that the women communicated to
Jesus' followers on Easter morning: *They went to the tomb early*

this morning but didn't find his body. They came and told us that they had seen a vision of angels, who said he was alive." Not surprisingly, the men who first hear these bewildering claims—a group that included our two friends on the Emmaus road—do not believe them.

It is not only the bizarre tale of a resurrection that produces skepticism among the disciples. The inferior status of women at the time makes their claim even less credible. Women were assumed to be less rational and trustworthy; their testimony was not even admitted into Jewish or Roman courts. Why in the world, these men must have asked themselves, would messengers from God entrust such urgent and momentous news *to women?* Their first thought is that someone had invaded the tomb and stolen the body. As for the story from these overwrought women, as Luke's account baldly admits, "their words seemed to them like nonsense."[26]

For many modern readers, their words still seem like nonsense. Yet the earliest historical records we have about the death of Jesus all agree on this point: within three days of his execution and burial, the tomb of Jesus was unoccupied.

As Oxford historian C. H. Dodd summarized the scene, the unchallenged assumption was that if anyone cared to visit the grave site, a short distance from the city center, he would find it empty: "The gospels supplement this by saying, it *was* visited, and it *was* found empty."[27] There is no scrap of evidence, either from religious or secular sources, that anyone even disputed the fact. Not even the critics and enemies of the early Christian church tried to produce a body. Thus, historians rightly regard the vacant tomb as "the one silent and infallible witness in the whole episode."[28]

Were angelic beings the first to announce this news? *"They came and told us that they had seen a vision of angels, who said he was alive."* The more important issue is whether there is room enough in our own minds to admit the possibility of the presence and activity of God. The women at the tomb of Jesus—for all their sorrows and fears—kept their hearts and minds open to grace. As a result, they helped launch the most potent and enduring revolution in the history of the world.

6

A DIVINE CONSPIRACY

"'How foolish you are, and how slow of
heart to believe all that the prophets have
spoken! Did not the Christ have to suffer
these things and then enter his glory?' And
beginning with Moses and all the Prophets,
he explained to them what was said in all the
Scriptures concerning himself."

---

*As the triumphant and charismatic general parades through the streets
of Rome, crowds of admirers abandon their day jobs to catch a glimpse
of him and cheer him on. He has conquered more armies and seized
more land than any ruler in the history of Rome.*

*Not everyone is an admirer. Cassius, a member of the Roman
Senate, watches the scene with growing anxiety. The general is quickly
consolidating his political power, and Cassius fears that Rome's republican government is in danger of becoming a dictatorship. "Why, man,
he doth bestride the narrow world / Like a Colossus," he complains,
"and we petty men / Walk under his huge legs and peep about / To find*

ourselves dishonourable graves."[1] Cassius is a man of ambition himself and is moved by jealousy more than patriotic duty. He hatches a plot to assassinate the general, the man known to history as Julius Caesar.

Now Cassius must convince loyal senators such as Brutus, with a reputation as a noble statesman, to join the conspiracy. Brutus at first is appalled at the prospect: "Where wilt thou find a cavern dark enough / To mask thy monstrous visage? Seek none, Conspiracy! / Hide it in smiles and affability . . ."[2] Yet soon enough Brutus is persuaded that the likelihood of tyrannical rule under Caesar is too great a risk.

At eight o'clock, on March 15, 44 BC, a cohort of conspirators escorts Caesar to the Senate. Suddenly, in a moment, they are on him with their knives, stabbing him again and again. Before the bloodbath is over, fifty-nine men join the act of assassination.

Although William Shakespeare based his play *Julius Caesar* on historical accounts of the assassination, he gave himself some literary license. We don't really know how the plot evolved or who all the key players were. But we do know that Caesar was hacked to death in an orgy of violence—twenty-three stab wounds—that shocked the sensibilities of ancient Rome. Shakespeare took that fact and wove a tale of intrigue, deception, betrayal, and murder that still captivates modern audiences.

Just about everybody loves a good conspiracy story, especially if it involves politics or organized religion—or both. In 2003, mystery author Dan Brown released *The Da Vinci Code*, a fanciful novel about the secret history of the Catholic Church. It became an international blockbuster. Brown has persuaded millions of readers that Christianity sits atop a vast institutional conspiracy, a romantic relationship between Jesus and Mary of Magdala that he claims has been hushed up for centuries by the Church.

"You can point to the alleged miracles of the Bible, or any other religious text," Brown explains, "but they are nothing but old stories fabricated by man and then exaggerated over time."[3] It is a message many people are apparently eager to believe. Translated into forty-four languages, *The Da Vinci Code* has sold over eighty million copies. That makes it one of the bestselling English-language novels of the twenty-first century.

Whatever we think about Brown's retelling of Christian history, there is a sense in which *The Da Vinci Code* is right. At the center of the Christian story there is, in fact, a startling conspiracy. It is a tale about a Secret Rescue Mission, more daring than any fiction writer could imagine.[4] It involves a vast web of co-conspirators, operating in exotic capitals as well as desert hideouts. There are spies, plots, oaths, betrayals, and assassinations. There are heroes and villains, narrow escapes, and heartbreaking failures.

Through it all is an urgent and transcendent message: God has worked behind the scenes of history, deep within culture and society—*incognito*—to reclaim the human race from a desperate tragedy of its own making.

Many people assume that the Bible is just another book about morality; the dos and don'ts for those who worry about their relationship with God. Who can blame them? Sloppy and legalistic preaching has done more to muddy the faith than any "Jesus Seminar" or apocalyptic thriller from Hollywood. There are, to be sure, many teachings in the Bible about what it means to love our neighbor, but they are not the main attraction. What unites all the books that make up the Scripture—what binds the Old and New Testaments together—is a singular, coherent story. It is the story of how a world of breathtaking beauty fell into ruin because of human selfishness. But God, because of his unshakeable love, prepared the world for his arrival in disguise, the arrival of a Rescuer.

This is the secret the stranger on the road to Emmaus reveals to our two companions: the Rescuer has arrived. His name is Jesus of Nazareth, the same figure referred to in the Hebrew Bible as "the hope of all the ends of the earth."[5] Hope incarnate has appeared among them. *"And beginning with Moses and all the Prophets, he explained to them what was said in all the Scriptures concerning himself."* As we shall see, the Christian story is indeed a conspiracy story—a divine conspiracy—and there is no one who is not implicated in its plot.[6]

The Popularity of Paranoia

Some will protest that conspiracy theories are part of the problem. One of the most destructive forces in the history of the West, after all, found inspiration in a vile conspiracy theory involving the Jews. It is known as the *Protocols of the Elders of Zion*, the alleged record of secret meetings held by the "twelve tribes of Israel" and led by a Grand Rabbi, whose purpose was to plan the takeover of the entire world.

The meetings never occurred. The pamphlet is a forgery created by the secret police of Imperial Russia. Used at first to implicate the Jews in the 1905 socialist revolution in Russia, the

Protocols found a greedy audience wherever it was distributed. During the 1920s and 1930s, international sales of the pamphlet skyrocketed. Henri Rollin, the French scholar of anti-Semitism, called the *Protocols* "the most widely distributed book in the world other than the Bible."[7]

A sampling of the tract instantly reveals its anti-Jewish paranoia. "It is from us that the all-engulfing terror proceeds. We have in our service persons of all opinions, of all doctrines, monarchists, demagogues, socialists, communists, and utopian dreamers of every kind. We have harnessed them all to the task: each one of them on his own account is boring away at the last remnants of authority, is striving to overthrow all established forms of order."[8] The *Protocols* became a favorite among members of Hitler's Nazi Party; it remains a popular book in much of the Middle East.

The problem of conspiracies goes way beyond anti-Semitism. Thanks to the World Wide Web and the growth of new media, anybody, at any moment, can disseminate his opinions, no matter how venal or absurd. Rather than being a force for knowledge and mutual understanding, the Internet is stoking the flames of paranoia and group identity. Everyone can escape into his own echo chamber of ignorance and intolerance.

The 9/11 Truth movement—sustained by an army of "truthers" who believe the terrorist attacks were orchestrated by the U.S. government—serves as Exhibit A. No matter how much evidence is presented, the "official version" of events is rejected. After three years interviewing conspiracy theorists, journalist Jonathan Kay saw a cultural crisis in the making. In his book *Among the Truthers*, Kay warns that a "gaping cognitive hole" has been created—a breakdown in trust in America's basic institutions—which is being filled by every breed of lunatic group imaginable. "When a critical mass of educated people in a society lose their grip on the real world . . . it is a signal that the ordinary rules of rational intellectual inquiry are now treated as optional."[9]

Whatever form a conspiracy theory takes, we cannot seem to get enough of them; even old theories are getting a fresh hearing. Here is a smattering of recent titles from the bookstores:

- *LBJ and the Conspiracy to Kill Kennedy: A Coalescence of Interests*
- *The NASA Conspiracies: The Truth Behind the Moon Landings*
- *American Brutus: John Wilkes Booth and the Lincoln Conspiracies*
- *The Terror Conspiracy: Deception, 9/11 and the Loss of Liberty*
- *The Trillion-Dollar Conspiracy: How the New World Order, Man-Made Diseases, and Zombie Banks Are Destroying America*
- *The Aquarian Conspiracy: Personal and Social Transformation in Our Time*
- *The Diana Conspiracy Exposed: The Definitive Account*
- *How I Accidentally Joined the Vast Right-Wing Conspiracy (and Found Inner Peace)*
- *Failure to Cure: A Health Care Conspiracy*
- *The Greener Grass Conspiracy: Finding Contentment on Your Side of the Fence*
- *The Michael Jackson Conspiracy*
- *The Glenn Miller Conspiracy: The Never-Before-Told Story of His Life—and Death*

I expected to find conspiracy books about JFK, Princess Diana, and Michael Jackson. But a conspiracy theory about Big Band leader Glenn Miller? Who in the world would want to murder a trombone player?

There is no simple psychological explanation for those who propagate conspiracy theories. Some are highly intelligent, restless contrarians who crave "the exhilarating sense of independence, control, and superiority" that comes with standing against conventional wisdom.[10] Others are ready to embrace any crackpot theory—or religion—that helps them cope with a troubling turn of events. Psychologists explain that such people are prone to look for connections where none actually exist. "Conspiracy theorists connect the dots of random events into meaningful patterns," writes behavioral psychologist Michael Shermer, "and then infuse those patterns with intentional agency."[11] In other words, they try to give meaning and purpose to events that seem to lack meaning or purpose.

Does this describe the emotional state of the disciples? Did they imagine divine intervention into the execution of Jesus in order to regain a sense of "control" or to help them make sense of it?

The two bewildered men on the Emmaus road, however, don't sound like control freaks. And we have already seen how their Jewish faith discouraged them from fantasizing that Jesus might somehow overcome death. Luke's version of events confirms this disposition: *"How foolish you are, and how slow of heart to believe all that the prophets have spoken!"* Their "heart" refers to their inner commitments, their willingness to take God at his word. The two friends are scolded, not for being conspiracy-mongers but for their *lack of faith.*

From the perspective of the stranger, they are skeptics about God's activity among the Jews and in the world at large. They are unwilling to "connect the dots" to discern the pattern and meaning of their own history.[12]

Disguise, Deceit, and Transformation

There is a difference, of course, between conspiracies and conspiracy theories. Although the latter are usually the product of overheated imaginations, the former may well be factual. Two thousand years ago there really was a conspiracy to assassinate Julius Caesar. Likewise, nearly a century ago there really was a plot to murder Austrian archduke Franz Ferdinand, the trigger event for the First World War. The scheme was organized by the Black Hand, a shadowy radical group committed to Serbian independence from the Austro-Hungarian Empire. Given the consequences of the war, it proved to be one of the most momentous conspiracies in modern history.

Wars and rumors of wars, in fact, are especially good breeding grounds for conspiracies. Maybe this is because there is so much at stake during a war: the fate of not only individuals but entire governments might depend on the outcome of a secret plot.

Take the popular British spy novel *The Thirty-Nine Steps*, written by John Buchan and made into a film by Alfred Hitchcock. The book recounts the adventures of Richard Hannay, an English gentleman bored to distraction by his life of leisure in London—until he becomes entangled in a plot to assassinate the Greek prime minister and instigate a European war. Wrongly accused of murder, Hannay finds himself pursued by both the police and the agents of the Black Stone, a conspiracy ring of German spies and assassins operating throughout the country.

Hannay learns that the ambitions of the Black Stone go far beyond a political assassination. Its goal is to capture plans for the location of the British Royal Navy in the event of war, giving Germany the ability to devastate the heart of Britain's military power and threaten its entire empire. The members of the Black Stone operate without boundaries, appearing in British cities as well as the most remote hamlets in the countryside. They pass themselves off as anonymous businessmen, leisurely gentlemen, and even government officials. In reality, they are ruthless killers indifferent to the human consequences of their actions.

The cunning and brutality of his enemies forces Hannay to fight them at least partly on their own terms. He uses disguise, deceit, and "an almost supernatural capacity for transformation."[13] To escape his London flat, he dresses as a milkman. On a train to Scotland, he takes a third-class carriage and poses as a poor Scottish hill farmer. To an innkeeper he becomes a South African mining magnate. He addresses a political rally as an Australian supporter of free trade. He poses as a roadman, sailor, and cattle herder.[14]

Through it all, through every threat and danger, Hannay keeps his motives pure and unselfish: to save Britain from military disaster and to prove his innocence. "Above all, I must keep going myself, ready to act when things get riper," he says, "and that was going to be no light job with the police of the British Isles in full cry after me and the watchers of the Black Stone running silently and swiftly on my trail."[15]

What makes the story so memorable, writes film critic Mark Glancy, is "the sense of menace lurking behind the façade of normality, the idea that the world stands on the brink of destruction and there is only one man who knows this and can save it."[16] It is something like this sense of menace that compels people to enter into another kind of conspiracy—a plot to rescue the innocent from great harm.

Conspirators for Human Freedom

The conspiracies I now have in mind are not of the *Julius Caesar* variety. They are not inspired by the lust to dominate but by a desire to liberate. Although in their tactics they may resemble destructive conspiracies—in their use of secrecy and deception, for example—the motives of these collaborators are completely different. They are prepared to sacrifice everything for the sake of others.

Some of the most riveting real-life examples of conspiracies of this kind occurred during the Second World War. One involved an assassination plot against Adolf Hitler, called Operation Valkyrie. Another involved the Allied invasion at Normandy, known as Operation Overlord. A third involved a resistance movement in occupied France. Let us look briefly at each of them, for they have their counterparts in the Christian story of rescue and liberation.

Valkyrie

It is hard to exaggerate the sense of triumph and euphoria among the Germans soon after Adolf Hitler came to power in 1933. Everything Hitler promised about the restoration of national pride, about revenge for the Treaty of Versailles, about the natural supremacy of the Aryan race—all of it was coming true. To the German people, and especially to the German military, it seemed that Hitler was a miracle worker.

To a small but growing number of German army officers, however, Hitler had become "evil incarnate." That is how Claus von Stauffenberg, a central figure in a conspiracy to assassinate Hitler, came to describe him. Stauffenberg and others had seen for themselves the atrocities committed by the Nazis—the murder of civilians, the torture and starvation of prisoners, the mass execution of Jews. "It's time now for something to be done," Stauffenberg declared. "He who has the courage to act must know that he will probably go down in German history as a traitor. But if he fails to act, he will be a traitor before his own conscience."

The plan, code-named "Valkyrie," was to set off a powerful bomb inside the Wolf's Lair, Hitler's headquarters in East Prussia, killing the *führer*. The officers would then seize control of the government in a coup.

The story of Stauffenberg and his coconspirators was made into a movie, *Valkyrie* (2008), with Tom Cruise in the lead role. One of the tensions in the film, faithful to the historical events, is the dilemma of the German officers, all of whom had sworn an oath of absolute loyalty to Hitler. Even talk of a military coup was considered a crime against the State. Nevertheless, Stauffenberg rebukes an officer who accuses him of treason for trying to recruit him to the cause. "Don't delude yourself," he warns. "You were involved in a crime against your country long before you met me. But there may still be time to redeem your soul."

A recurring motif in *Valkyrie* is the absolute necessity for people to make a choice for or against the conspiracy. This is powerfully dramatized during a scene in a communications center in Berlin. Hitler is believed to be dead, and a military coup is underway. But there are conflicting messages being received about who is in command—some from forces loyal to the *führer*, others from the conspirators. Finally, an officer appeals to his commander: "It's a coup all right. We can't afford to remain neutral any longer. You have to make a decision. But when it's over, we better wind up on the right side."

The Valkyrie conspirators made the most fateful decision of their lives: they chose to submit their wills not to the State, but to their conscience. "Let's get to the heart of the matter," Stauffenberg told fellow conspirator Axel von dem Bussche. "I am committing high treason with all my might and main." After several botched attempts, Stauffenberg delivered a bomb to Hitler's headquarters on July 20, 1944. The device went off as planned, but Hitler survived the blast.

With Hitler still alive, the coup attempt collapsed. The Gestapo rounded up more than seven thousand people. Nearly five thousand were executed, including almost all of the Valkyrie conspirators.

Deception on D-Day

Once Nazi Germany launched its *blitzkrieg* in Europe, the fate of democracy in the West was thrown into doubt. Nations fell like dead trees before the German military machine. By the summer of 1940, virtually every European state, with the exception of Great Britain, had succumbed to Nazi rule. France, despite having the largest army in Europe, collapsed within a matter of weeks.

Even after the United States entered the war in December 1941, there was no clear way forward to defeat Germany. Hitler had established a series of fortifications along the coastline of northern France—the so-called Atlantic Wall—to prevent an Allied attack. Yet an invasion across the English Channel into German-held territory had to be attempted. Plans for an assault at Normandy were drawn up. The date was set for the first week in June 1944.

The Allies had to convince the Germans that if an invasion force came, it would arrive at Calais—about 150 miles east of the actual invasion. There was no other way to prevent Hitler from rebuffing the Allied forces during their most vulnerable moment, on the beaches of northern France. But how?

By creating a phoney invasion force. Thus began the most elaborate conspiracy of deception in the history of modern warfare.

Thousands of dummy inflatable tanks, artillery, and landing craft were deposited in fields in England opposite Calais. German reconnaissance planes were allowed to fly nearby, unhindered, to photograph them. The Allied Signal Corps transmitted a barrage of bogus radio messages about the invasion. U.S. general George S. Patton was given command of a fictional First U.S. Army Group, pretending to assemble a massive force. The Allies even dressed the corpse of a drowned British civilian in a military uniform, put him in a disabled plane off the coast of Portugal, and arranged for false maps and invasion plans to be found by German agents.

"It would not be proper even now to describe all the methods employed to mislead the enemy," wrote British prime minister Winston Churchill, shortly after the war. "The final result was admirable."[17]

Indeed it was. Historians credit the decoy operation with helping to confuse the Germans and minimize the Allied casualties at Normandy. It thus was crucial to the success of the entire Allied invasion of France on D-Day, June 6, 1944, the turning point in the war. Operation Overlord involved a massive international conspiracy to deceive a vicious and implacable enemy—and it worked.

France's Secret Army

While the Allied Forces were preparing for the invasion at Normandy, a group of French nationals were conspiring to disrupt the German occupation. After France surrendered to Nazi Germany in June 1940, a puppet government under a new French prime minister was set up at Vichy, in the southern part of the country. But thousands of ordinary French citizens, led by Charles de Gaulle, an officer in the French army, refused to take part in the surrender. They never gave up the hope of liberation. The French Resistance movement—later known as "France's Secret Army"—was born.

It was a people's army if ever there was one. Telephone workers formed a secret organization to sabotage telephone lines and disrupt military messages. Postal workers intercepted communications. Railroad workers destroyed tracks, blew up bridges, and diverted or derailed freight trains. The armed wing of the movement staged guerrilla attacks on the German military. By the time of Operation Overlord, the French Resistance numbered in the tens of thousands. It played a vital role in preventing German troops from engaging the Allies at Normandy. "As always, these resistance efforts were not without cost," writes historian Don Lawson. "The Germans were now desperate, and their reprisals were even more savage than before."[18]

Members of the Resistance learned to function in a culture of deception. They operated in a midnight existence of code names, false identities, secret orders—and betrayal. "We lived in the shadows as soldiers of the night, but our lives were not dark," writes Resistance leader Jean-Pierre Levy. "There were arrests, torture, and death for so many of our friends and comrades, and tragedy awaited all of us just around the corner. But we did not live in or with tragedy. We were exhilarated by the challenge and rightness of our cause."[19]

An estimated 56,000 French Resistance fighters were exposed, captured, and sent to concentration camps before the end of the war. Half of them never returned.

The Mother of All Conspiracies

Not all conspiracies, then, are to be despised. Each of these war-time conspiracies involved a great contest between the defenders of civilization and the forces of barbarism. The conspirators could not predict how their efforts might affect the outcome of the conflict. Despite their virtuous motives, they were beset by ambiguities. None of them could be sure their cause would prevail. But there was no doubt they were part of a much larger story—the ancient struggle between tyranny and freedom.

In this sense, each of these plots against Nazism is reminiscent of the astonishing story that is unfolding on the road to Emmaus. *"'Did not the Christ have to suffer these things and then enter his glory?' And beginning with Moses and all the Prophets, he explained to them what was said in all the Scriptures concerning himself."* The stranger confronts the disciples with a new account of "the Christ," the Greek term for the Hebrew *Messiah*, the Rescuer of Israel.[20] They are about to learn how the entire history of the Jewish people can be understood—even more, *must* be understood—by his promised arrival.

The meaning of the divine conspiracy, an ancient mystery about God and the great battle for the world he has made, is about to be disclosed.

We have already seen how the popular view of the Messiah—a person of immense supernatural power, a political liberator, a divinely anointed king—created a crisis of faith for the disciples. They dared to hope that Jesus of Nazareth might be this promised Messiah. But they cannot accept the idea of a Messiah who suffers defeat, much less a criminal's death on a cross. Yet it is precisely this idea that the stranger presses upon them. Conventional wisdom about the Messiah is about to be tossed into the trash heap.

What exactly does he tell them? The Hebrew Scripture is the key to unlocking this mystery about God's activity in the world. For observant Jews, in the first century as well as today, the writings of Moses and the Prophets are the nearest things to the mind of God in human language. "If God is alive, then the Bible is His voice," writes Jewish thinker Abraham Heschel. "No other work is as worthy of being considered a manifestation of His will. There is no other mirror in the world where His will and spiritual guidance is as unmistakably reflected."[21]

It is to this book, and no other, that the stranger immediately takes his listeners. What does he tell them? We are not given the details, but we can guess from the preaching of the early church what was said to them on the Emmaus road. From the opening pages of the Bible, the two friends are reminded of the fierce and unfaltering love of God for the world he has made. His divine love burns hotter than any star in the universe. Here is love that is never lazy, indulgent, or indifferent but always vigilant—committed to the perfect good of the beloved.

The stranger describes the deep enmity that has rejected this love and spoiled the world, the rage of those who will not yield their hearts to their Creator. Men and women, made to love God and to enjoy him forever, somehow succumbed to the forces of deceit and darkness set against him, symbolized by a serpent. "You will be like God," the serpent whispered.[22] Instead, they became captives to the suffocating selfishness of a life cut off from God's goodness. No one, the stranger insists, no matter what his status or achievements in the world, can escape this state of affairs. It would remain the burden and the blight of human beings everywhere in every age—unless a Rescuer were sent to set them free.

It is here, in the early pages of Genesis, where we first learn of the Rescuer and his mission to the world. He will confront the leader of the forces of darkness, the Deceiver, also known as the devil. He will be grievously wounded. Yet in the end, he will overcome the Deceiver and the hatreds unleashed upon the earth. "The Rescuer will crush your head," God tells the serpent, "and you will strike his heel."[23]

This is God's Secret Rescue Mission to the world. Of all the nations of the earth, the stranger explains, God chose one nation—the people of Israel—to help him accomplish this mission.

Yet just as men and women became slaves to spiritual

darkness, God's chosen nation also found itself in bondage, held captive by a despotic king in Egypt. The Jews cried out to God to rescue them, and he heard their cries. As Moses wrote in the book of Exodus, God sent an Angel of Death to kill all the firstborn children in Egypt, to compel its wicked leader to free the Jews from their oppressors. All the firstborn in every family would die! There was only one way for a family to escape death: they must cover their doorframe with the blood of a sacrificed lamb. "The blood will be a sign for you on the houses where you are," God tells his people, "and when I see the blood, I will pass over you. No destructive plague will touch you when I strike Egypt."[24]

To their bewilderment, the stranger reveals that the Messiah, the Rescuer, would be like this "Passover lamb." *He was to be sacrificed to save others from the awful judgment of God.* These men had read and recited the words of Moses and the Prophets from childhood. They had never failed to observe the Passover meal, not once. Yet somehow they had not understood the message about a Messiah who suffers for the sins of Israel in order to bring God's people everlasting freedom.

The stranger reminds them of the wrenching cry of David in the Psalms: "Dogs surround me; a pack of villains encircles me; they pierce my hands and my feet. . . . They divide my clothes among them and cast lots for my garments."[25] He quotes from Isaiah's description of a servant of God who brings true healing and forgiveness: "But he was pierced for our transgressions, he was crushed for our iniquities; the punishment that brought us peace was on him."[26] He recalls the many warnings from the Prophets about a darker judgment than being exiled from the promised land and a more glorious salvation than returning to it.

It seems impossible to believe: this figure of suffering is the promised Rescuer of Israel. He is the last prophet from the family tree of King David, born in the same place as David, the town of Bethlehem. The history of Israel, they learn, is a story of preparation for his coming.

As the stranger continues, the men remember what they felt the first time they heard Jesus speak.[27] It was in a synagogue in Nazareth, where he stood up and read from Isaiah: "The Spirit of the Lord is on me, because he has anointed me to proclaim good news to the poor. He has sent me to proclaim freedom for the prisoners and recovery of sight for the blind, to set the oppressed free, to proclaim the year of the Lord's favor."[28] They remembered how their hearts throbbed with hope—the hope that God was finally at work again in Israel. And then, as if to confirm their secret thoughts, Jesus declared to all of them: "Today this scripture is fulfilled in your hearing."[29]

God in Disguise

This is the divine conspiracy that has been in the mind of God almost from the beginning. In a sense, it is not very different from other conspiracies that have appeared in history. Like them, it has inspired magnificent heroism, as well as wretched betrayals. It has sparked wars and created exiles. In its cause it has deployed spies and assassins, soldiers and clerks, mothers and prostitutes. The steadfast march of its purpose has toppled kings and determined the fate of nations. Even so, its consummation depends not on the will of powerful men, but on the appearance of a helpless baby, born to a poor Jewish girl in a cramped stable on a cold night, a night as quiet as falling snow.

"You will conceive and give birth to a son, and you are to call him Jesus. He will be great and will be called the Son of the Most High," an angel told his mother. "The Lord God will give him the throne of his father David, and he will reign over the house of Jacob forever; his kingdom will never end."[30]

Is this not the greatest conspiracy story ever conceived?

If what the stranger says is true, then for many of us, like the disciples on the Emmaus road, our view of God's relationship to our world—and our relationship to him—faces a severe test. The God who spoke the universe into existence has entered the world of flesh and blood for one purpose: to save it. He has been at work among us, carrying out a mission of rescue and redemption that we never imagined. All effective conspiracies share this quality of surprise. The plot itself, and the people involved in it, are not suspected.

This is one of the great themes of Tolkien's *The Lord of the Rings*. The characters chosen to undertake the desperate mission to Mount Doom, Frodo Baggins and Sam Gamgee, seem the least likely to succeed, homely hobbits who would prefer to remain in the comfort of the Shire. Even more, the heroic quest to which they devote themselves, the destruction of the Ring, would seem like nonsense to their enemies—if they ever dared to consider it.

But this they cannot do. For the Ring is an object of great power, lusted after by Sauron and all the dark forces of Mordor. As Gandalf explains to his companions: "That we should try to destroy the Ring itself has not yet entered into his darkest dream."[31] W. H. Auden, in an early review of Tolkien's trilogy, put it this way: "Good can imagine the possibility of becoming evil—hence the refusal of Gandalf and Aragorn to use the

Ring—but Evil, defiantly chosen, can no longer imagine anything but itself."[32]

The thought that anyone who possessed ultimate power would give it up for some selfless purpose—out of love for another—does not easily penetrate the mind of the wicked. But if the stranger's words to the disciples are true, this is precisely what God, in the Person of Jesus, has done for every man and woman who has ever lived.

Are we prepared to allow this thought to enter our minds?

7

OUR INCONSOLABLE SECRET

"When he was at the table with them, he took bread, gave thanks, broke it and began to give it to them. Then their eyes were opened and they recognized him, and he disappeared from their sight. They asked each other, 'Were not our hearts burning within us while he talked with us on the road and opened the Scriptures to us?'"

———◆———

It is the fifth inning of a game between the Baltimore Orioles and the California Angels, and the sense of anticipation is almost unbearable. An unassailable record is about to be shattered. The date is September 6, 1995, a moment in the history of baseball that seems to reach beyond time, beyond baseball, beyond anything most anyone watching the game has ever experienced.

Over the previous fifteen years, Orioles shortstop Cal Ripken has showed up for work every day, without complaint, without fail. He loves his craft, the craft of the professional ballplayer. Neither injuries nor illness can keep him off the field. And so, without ever intending it, he has played in 2,130 consecutive games—a nearly superhuman record first set by legendary New York Yankee Lou Gehrig. The record has stood, unchallenged, for fifty-six years. It has become a symbol of grit, perseverance, and selfless dedication. No one in baseball ever imagined it might be broken.

But tonight tens of thousands of fans have crowded into Camden Yards to watch Ripken surpass Gehrig's achievement. He gives them a night to remember. In the fourth inning, when Ripken slams a home run over the left field fence, the crowd is simultaneously stunned and exuberant. And then, in the middle of the fifth inning, when the game becomes official, a numerical banner displaying the 2,130 mark changes to 2,131.

The capacity crowd at Camden Yards rises to its feet and remains there for twenty-two minutes, giving Ripken one of the longest standing ovations in sports history. It is a thunderous, unbroken expression of praise. Members of the opposing team, as well as all four umpires, join them.

The modest Ripken is uncomfortable with all the attention and uneasy about the game being delayed. Teammates Bobby Bonilla and Rafael Palmeiro playfully shove him out of the dugout, insisting that he take a victory lap. "Hey, if you don't do a lap around this thing," they tell him, "we'll never get the game started."

Unlike most ballplayers, Ripken has remained with the team that first hired him—the Baltimore Orioles—for his entire career. His family has deep roots in the city and in the Orioles club. Ripken has never imagined playing for any other team. He knows many of the fans and their families personally; some of his friends make a point of seeing him play whenever the O's are in town.

So this victory lap is not about a celebrity tipping his hat to a faceless multitude. It becomes something deeply personal, a kind of family reunion. Ripken shakes hands, embraces old friends, thanks people by name. "I started seeing people I knew," he explained. "Those were the people that had been around the ballpark all those years, and it was really a wonderful human experience."[1]

A commentator marvelled at the thousands of hands outstretched toward Ripken: "He was being more than cheered. This was adoration."[2]

———◦•◦———

Some of the most ennobling human experiences are those in which we honor individuals not for their star status, but for their character—when quiet decency, faithfulness, or heroism almost demands our praise. A mother's tenderness toward her newborn baby, a friend who stands by us in our deepest struggle, a passerby who charges into a burning house to rescue a child—who is not moved by these acts of sacrifice?

Even as spectators, we find that such experiences can yank us loose from our preoccupations, if only for a moment. They lift us out of ourselves. They allow us to hear what C. S. Lewis called the "shy, persistent, inner voice . . . a desire which no natural happiness will satisfy."[3] Suddenly, unexpectedly, we long to live in a different world than the one we know. "He looks again," writes Dante, "and to himself he swears that God intended something new for earth."[4]

Is it this sense of longing that seizes our two friends on their way to Emmaus?

Soon after they arrive in the village, they will recognize the stranger who has joined them on their journey. Faith will fully awaken within them, and it will transform them. While they are on the road, however, they still do not apprehend who he is—and yet something he has told them is provoking them: *"Were not our hearts burning within us while he talked with us on the road and opened the Scriptures to us?"*

What is it? And what effect is this knowledge having on their hearts and minds? The stranger has led them to the Scripture to help them see how God has been faithful to the people of Israel. He has revealed to them a profound mystery, not only about the Jewish people but about the destiny of the human race. He has laid bare God's Secret Rescue Mission for mankind.

All their lives these men have lived with a burden of fear and struggle and oppression. Now, for the first time, they see clearly a vision of the world they were meant to live in—a world without fear, sorrow, or suffering, where justice and mercy make their home together. All their lives they have been taught to think only of their obligations to God, the commandments he has given them, and the penalties for breaking them. Here is a place where only the pure in heart may dwell: those whose faces are "fair and young and fearless and full of joy."[5]

This is how Jesus spoke of the kingdom of heaven when he was with them in Galilee, Judea, and Jerusalem. It is the kingdom they have been longing for all their lives—they know it in their hearts, and this knowledge begins to change them.

The Quest for a Just Society

Thus we encounter another of those remarkable facts about this conversation on the Emmaus road and the human condition. For it is something very close to this vision of human life—of how life *ought* to be—that has haunted the imagination of the West from its earliest days.

We find hints of this among the Greeks, who sought to create a more just and virtuous society, in contrast to the tyrannies that dominated the ancient world. Somehow they acquired the radical idea that dictatorships were illegitimate because they violated human nature, that people were made to live in freedom, not ruled by force. The Greeks wanted a political system in which they could govern themselves, where the people (the *demos*) had access to power (*kratos*). Their vision of a just society was a *demokratia*. The Athenian statesman Solon called this the "sacred foundation of justice."[6]

So the Greeks dispensed with their tyrants. In Athens, the murder of Hipparchus in 514 marked the beginning of the "cult of the tyrannicides"—individuals who committed themselves to assassinating tyrants.[7] This paved the way for the political reforms of Cleisthenes, the father of Athenian democracy. The Greeks took immense pride in their system of self-government. Their leading statesman, Pericles, lauded his nation's ideals in a speech honoring those who had fallen in battle. It is often called the Gettysburg Address of Greece:

> It is true that we are called a democracy, for the administration is in the hands of the many and not of the few. But while there exists equal justice to all and alike in their private disputes, the claim of excellence is also recognized; and when a citizen is in any way distinguished, he is preferred to the public service, not as a matter of privilege, but as the reward of merit. Neither is poverty an obstacle, but a man may benefit his country whatever the obscurity of his condition . . . We alone do good to our neighbors not upon a calculation of interest, but in the confidence of freedom and in a frank and fearless spirit.[8]

In their pursuit of a more just society—"equal justice to all"—the people of Athens established a political constitution that was as thoroughly democratic as the world has ever seen. The rest of the ancient world would be ruled by dictatorships, monarchies, tyrannies. But in Athens, democracy—the idea of government by consent of the governed—was taken as far as it would go before modern times.

Not everyone believed that Athenian democracy would produce a better society. Plato's *The Republic*, one of the foundational political texts of the West, was a stunning rebuke to the entire Greek project. In it, Plato offered his own vision of earthly justice. A truly just society could only be brought about, he argued, by an enlightened cohort of philosopher-kings, groomed from infancy to rule righteously. "We want no scoundrels governing us. Our purpose is to create true guardians of our liberties, men least likely to do the city harm," he writes. "The city we have founded—if we have built rightly—will be good in the fullest sense of the word."[9]

Greek democracy collapsed, of course, and the republic imagined by Plato never saw the light of day. Yet the dream of a society governed with justice and equity was kept alive by a new superpower in the ancient world: Rome. Here is how the poet Virgil described Rome's exalted mission among the nations of the earth:

> Roman, remember by your strength to rule Earth's peoples—for your arts are to be these: to pacify, to impose the rule of law, to spare the conquered, battle down the proud.[10]

It was the Roman emperor Augustus, more than any other, who devoted himself to implementing Virgil's vision. During his forty-year reign, he helped transform Rome into a world capital. He sought to teach the Romans to identify their destiny with the destiny of all mankind. They alone were the chosen people who would bring peace and stability to a violent, terrifying, and uncertain world. Whereas the Greeks were focused on their individual city-states, the Romans looked outward to a universal empire. The aim of the *Pax Romana*, or Roman Peace, wasn't simply to subdue other peoples, but to realize a new kind of civilization, a global political regime that promoted a just and virtuous society.

The Roman Empire—with its militarism, slavery, and political violence—fell far short of its ideals. But compared to the barbarian tribes wandering much of Europe, Roman rule looked pretty good. Inhabitants from the farthest reaches of the empire wanted to become Roman citizens. For them, Rome was the world. For all its brutalities, it was synonymous with order, security, and power. Thus the Romans famously built a network of roads and bridges stretching 53,000 miles to bind its conquered peoples into a civilized, coherent, and universal society.

The epic film *Gladiator* (2000), directed by Ridley Scott, captures something of this vision. Early in the story is a moving exchange between Marcus Aurelius, the Roman emperor, and Maximus, a loyal general. Surprisingly, the emperor expresses doubts about the meaning of his empire building. It is a fictional exchange, but it offers a glimpse into Rome's self-understanding of its global mission:

A: Do you see that map, Maximus? That is the world which I created. For twenty-five years I have conquered, spilled blood, expanded the empire. Since I became caesar, I have known four years without war . . . for what?

M: Five thousand of my men are out there on the freezing mud. Three thousand of them are bloodied. Two thousand of them will never leave this place. I will not believe that they fought and died for nothing!

A: Then what would you believe?

M: They fought for you . . . and for Rome.

A: And what is Rome, Maximus?

M: I have seen much of the rest of the world. It is brutal and cruel and dark. Rome is the light.

This is how Rome's leaders, and probably most of its citizens, thought about their empire. The world outside its borders was black with barbarism, random violence, grinding poverty, hopelessness. Rome was different. Here, and nowhere else, was civilization: a government that upheld rights, laws, order, religion, and virtue. Rome held out the promise of a just society in a world of injustice and cruelty.

With darkness all around, Rome was the light.

The Hope of Transformation

Why is this history important? Because it reminds us that there is something common to human societies everywhere, lodged deep in our DNA, that reaches anxiously for a world outside of our actual experience, something not quite of this earth.

Even a glance at the record of humanity's struggles—the wars, revolutions, assassinations, constitutions, conspiracies—reveals our relentless ambition for a society that has achieved the highest degree of justice and peace. The early Marxists dreamed of a "worker's paradise," a world without poverty or want. The French Revolutionaries believed their new regime would establish "the natural, inalienable and sacred rights of man."[11] The American Founders called their republic "a new order for the ages." The architects of the United Nations designed a global community to "save succeeding generations from the scourge of war."[12]

It would be easy to dismiss these impulses as mere utopianism, the musings of dreamers who appear in every society in every age. But surely there is something deeper at work. C. S. Lewis detected a universal desire—expressed in our culture, as well as our politics—to bridge a chasm that stretches between us and this other reality. From the perspective of faith, Lewis understood this reality as heaven itself, our true home. "Apparently, then, our lifelong nostalgia, our longing to be reunited with something in the universe from which we now feel cut off . . . is no mere neurotic fancy, but the truest index of our real situation." Lewis called this perpetual longing "our inconsolable secret."[13]

Why are we so restless for a world that seems to exist only in our imagination? Could it be that part of what draws us—what whispers to us in our conscience—is the hope that in this new world we might become new people?

"We are engaged in a great struggle, a struggle greater than it seems," warned Plato. "The issue is whether we shall become good or bad." Plato went further, suggesting that the soul's desire for virtue—what might be called moral beauty—was bound up with a desire for God. "We must disclose the yearning that links it to the immortal and divine and . . . we must discover what it would become if it gave itself wholly to what it yearns for."[14]

What would it be like if we gave ourselves fully to this desire for goodness?

Years ago I read about a group of filmgoers at a theater in New York City, surrendering nine dollars a head—not to see a movie, but a 2.5-minute trailer. The film was *The Phantom Menace*, the latest installment in the *Star Wars* franchise after a lengthy production hiatus. Chris Bergoch, a twenty-six-year-old *Star Wars* fan, took the day off from work and got to the theater at 10:00 a.m. By 8:00 p.m., he had seen the trailer twenty times and was planning to stay the rest of the night. As Bergoch put it: "I've waited 16 years for this."[15]

It is easy to write this off as pure escapism, to forget the powerful appeal of the *Star Wars* franchise. At one level, of course, it's a good-versus-evil story. But at another level it is a story about transformation, and what even the possibility of transformation can do. Luke Skywalker is driven by the hope that the Force will be with him, always, that he'll swing a light saber and slice Darth Vader like salami, that he will become something he is not—a Jedi Knight. Skywalker carries within him the hope of transformation—and so do we. "I've waited 16 years for this." Even watching it happen to someone else is powerful stuff.

What is it like to yield to this calling on our lives, to choose bravery, honesty, or purity when the moment of testing arrives? Whether in fiction or in real life, we are strangely attracted to individuals who submit themselves to this calling, especially in the throes of a great trial or contest. Let's remember a few of them together.

The Lady with the Lamp

Consider the story of a young nurse at the outbreak of the Crimean War. In 1853 Russia squared off against France and Britain over control of the Ottoman Empire. The conflict proved to be the bloodiest of the century, and gruesome reports of the conditions of the wounded began filtering back to Great Britain. On October 21, 1854, a head nurse and a team of thirty-eight women volunteers set sail for Istanbul—339 miles across the Black Sea—to treat British soldiers. The leader of the team—a headstrong, thirty-four-year-old daughter of privilege—was Florence Nightingale.

What she finds when she arrives is beyond description. Soldiers, untreated, lay dying not only from their wounds but from typhoid, cholera, and dysentery. There is a desperate lack of supplies. Nevertheless, Nightingale gets to work immediately, establishing sanitation, procuring medicines, making ward rounds daily. Historian Jacques Barzun observed that the stricken soldiers—up to five thousand at a time—soon regard her as "a saint, an angel sent to save their lives."[16]

Here is how a reporter on the scene for the *Times* newspaper described her work:

> As her slender form glides quietly along each corridor, every poor fellow's face softens with gratitude at the sight of her. When all the medical officers have retired for the night and silence and darkness have settled down upon those miles of prostrate sick, she may be observed alone, with a little lamp in her hand, making her solitary rounds.[17]

What caused Florence Nightingale, a woman born into an upper-class British family, to leave behind a life of ease and hurl herself into a swamp of human misery? A journal entry she wrote during a trip to Cairo offers a partial answer: "God called me in the morning and asked me, would I do good for him alone without reputation."[18] Something, it seems, spoke into Nightingale's conscience. Was it a glimpse of a world healed of its suffering? Her relentless work on behalf of the sick transformed the role of the nurse—at the time a menial and despised occupation—into a respected, professional vocation. She would not rest while others were in need. In the army barracks at Istanbul, she could be seen on her feet for twenty hours at a stretch.

They called her "the Lady with the Lamp."

The Last Full Measure of Devotion

Thanks to a soaring, lyrical, transcendent speech by Abraham Lincoln, most everyone knows something about the Battle of Gettysburg. Lesser known is the struggle for Little Round Top. It is the story of three hundred soldiers and a commander who led them in a desperate battle.

The day is July 2, 1863, two years into a civil war that has linked the fate of the United States to the institution of slavery. Confederate soldiers are engaging the Union Army on steep and rocky terrain two miles south of Gettysburg, on a hill known as Little Round Top. Union troops, under the command of Col. Joshua Lawrence Chamberlain, have seized the high ground. If you visit Gettysburg and climb to Little Round Top, you immediately see its tactical importance.

Chamberlain has only three hundred men at his command. Forming the extreme flank of the Union Army, his regiment, the 20th Main, is outnumbered ten to one. They are being battered. They face a Confederate force led by the almost mythical, and seemingly invincible, General Robert E. Lee. If Chamberlain's men falter—if they abandon their position in a panic—the Rebels will seize the high ground and advance up the flank of the Union army. If Lee's troops are successful, they could march on Philadelphia, or perhaps even Washington, D.C. Chamberlain's orders are clear: at all costs, hold your ground.

Chamberlain, whose great-grandfathers were soldiers in the Revolutionary War, understands both the military significance and the moral importance of the moment. After fending off a second assault by Confederate troops, Chamberlain and his men find themselves out of ammunition. Yet his resolve is like iron. He believes firmly in the cause of abolition. He holds a vision of a nobler America, a nation committed to human freedom, and it takes hold of him in the moment of crisis.

"Stand firm you boys from Maine," Chamberlain tells them, "for not once in a century are men permitted to bear such responsibilities for freedom and justice, for God and humanity, as are now placed upon you."[19] Chamberlain gives the order: fix bayonets.

The three hundred charge *down* Little Round Top, with bayonets mounted on their rifles, into the teeth of the Confederate Army. It is an audacious gamble. Rebel troops, stunned by the advance, fall back. Soon they are overwhelmed, hundreds are captured, and the Union Army holds the high ground. The fight for Little Round Top is the turning point in a battle that proves to be the turning point in the war.

As Lincoln would describe their sacrifice at Gettysburg, they gave "the last full measure of devotion" in order that "this nation, under God, shall have a new birth of freedom."

Always Ready to Help

No period was darker for European Jews than the final years of the Second World War, when Hitler's Germany was carrying out its "final solution" to the Jewish problem. By the end of the war, the Nazis had murdered six million Jews—a campaign of systematic extermination for which there was no moral category. Part of the tragedy of this period was the fact that the Nazis found so many willing collaborators. From every country under German occupation, Jews were identified, arrested, and shipped off to concentration camps.

Villagers in a poor mountain hamlet in France stood against this tide of criminality and murder. During four deranged and destitute years, 1940 to 1944, the entire village of Le Chambon-sur-Lignon opened its homes, farms, and cellars to Jews on the run. All told, they managed to rescue about thirty-five hundred Jews, all of whom survived the war. "In the midst of our struggle for survival . . . we creatures on earth have made room for thoughts and deeds of love," writes philosopher Philip Hallie, who uncovered their story. "Some creatures have made more room than others."[20]

Why did the residents of Le Chambon make room in their hearts for the Jewish refugees among them? There was, after all, hardly enough food or clothing for themselves. There was the constant threat of exposure, and the penalty for hiding a Jew was often death. Many hundreds of non-Jews across Europe were executed for offering help.

What compelled these villagers to act? Put simply, it was love that moved them—the love of Jesus. It was the Christian ideal of compassion, taught from the pulpit and lived out in family and community life. Led by Protestant minister André Trocmé and his wife, Magda, the villagers of Le Chambon bound themselves to serve the Jews among them, regardless of the risks. The believers from this Protestant village considered the Bible a book of absolute truths and commandments—not mere opinion and suggestion—to be obeyed no matter what the cost. "The word of God had to be taken that way or not at all," writes Hallie. "The felt allegiance of the Chambonnais to God's words convinced them in their heart of hearts that they were doing God's work by protecting the apple of God's eye, the Jews."

The villagers had a saying: *Toujours prêt a server*—always ready to help. "I experienced one of the greatest shocks of my life," writes Hallie, "when I realized that such an undramatic thing as the habit of helping was the living core of the rescue operation of Le Chambon."

Working with other French villages, the Chambonnais sustained the most effective Jewish rescue mission in France under the Nazis. Historian Sir Martin Gilbert, who has written extensively about the Holocaust and the Second World War, records his own amazement at their accomplishment: "The story of these villages is a high point in the narrative of rescue."[21]

Surprised by Joy

It is difficult to read stories like these—stories of healing, courage, and rescue—and not feel profoundly humbled by the people involved. We become aware of our own shortcomings, our petty concerns, our prejudices, our fears, our massive egos.

At the same time, something in most of us draws our hearts toward these individuals and everything they represent.

Just before Philip Hallie discovered the story of the Chambonnais, he was in a state of deep depression. He had finished researching and writing a book about cruelty, and for weeks afterward he was tormented by the stories of torture and killing. Fear, bitterness, and fury filled his soul. But when he finished reading an account of resistance among the villagers—a scene in which they openly defied French police by sheltering Jews—he found that his cheeks were awash in tears. "What had wrung these tears from me, body and soul, the way you squeeze a grape, seeds and all, to get its juice, though the seeds make the juice bitter?" he asked. "It was joy that did it, overwhelming joy, which can squeeze tears out of us as suddenly as misery can."[22]

We all experience for ourselves moments like this, when moral beauty rises before our eyes like a mountain peak beyond a dense and dark wood. What follows in that moment is joy, inexpressible and nearly irresistible.

We are getting closer to understanding what has seized the hearts of the two disciples on the Emmaus road. *They asked each other, 'Were not our hearts burning within us while he talked with us on the road and opened the Scriptures to us?'* When Jesus walked among these men, they were captivated by his description of the kingdom of heaven and the promise of Israel restored. They were delighted by his stories of God's love for the lowly, people maligned even by their own religious leaders. But now their attention is drawn not simply to Israel, not to a new religious morality, not even to God's kingdom, but to a person—the Messiah. It is to him, the Rescuer, that the stranger has directed their minds, and they are nearly overcome with joy.

Seventeen centuries later another follower of Jesus, a brilliant composer, would share in this experience. His name was Johann Sebastian Bach. Because of the bold declarations of Christian faith in his music, he is often called "the fifth Evangelist" among Church historians. "The aim and final reason of all music should be none else but the glory of God and refreshing the soul," he once wrote. "Where this is not observed there will be no music, but only a devilish hubbub."[23] Contemporary artists would take issue with Bach on this point. Nevertheless, take note at the next wedding ceremony you attend. You're more likely to hear Bach's anthem of praise, "Jesu, Joy of Man's Desiring," than, say, Lady Gaga's "The Edge of Glory."

> Jesu, joy of man's desiring,
> Holy wisdom, love most bright;
> Drawn by Thee, our souls aspiring
> Soar to uncreated light. . . .
> Through the way where hope is guiding,
> Hark, what peaceful music rings;
> Where the flock, in Thee confiding,
> Drink of joy from deathless springs.
> Theirs is beauty's fairest pleasure;
> Theirs is wisdom's holiest treasure.
> Thou dost ever lead Thine own
> In the love of joys unknown.[24]

What Bach accomplished with music, Rembrandt expressed in painting. Regarded as "the greatest artist of the age," he was another creative genius who counted himself among the followers of Jesus.[25] No artist in his day painted more scenes from the

Bible or was more determined to probe the moral and spiritual condition of man. Thanks to some dear friends and art buffs from Philadelphia, I got a chance to see a special collection of his work at the Philadelphia Museum of Art.[26] Rembrandt's intimate oil sketches of the face of Jesus—emphasizing the qualities of empathy and grace—are considered masterpieces of interpretation that transformed the history of Christian art. "He was alone with his experience of life, which he had to lift on to a spiritual plane without any sacrifice of truth, and with no other guidance than the words of the Bible," writes historian Kenneth Clark. Rembrandt, he said, "digs down deep to the roots of life."[27]

Rembrandt's many renderings of the encounter on the road to Emmaus, based on his "careful reading of the Gospels," reflect the nuances in Luke's record of the exchange.[28] The men seem transfixed yet puzzled at the same time. The stranger walks with them like any other man, yet there is something luminous about him. Like Luke's account, Rembrandt's depictions leave us with no reason to think they have been hallucinating or that they are in the presence of some ghostly apparition.

The disciples are deeply affected by their conversation with the stranger. Nevertheless, they still do not recognize him; they do not perceive that they are in the presence of Jesus himself. Something keeps them from understanding what has happened. Something else is required, it seems, before belief in a risen Jesus finally takes hold.

A Meal—and a Moment of Enlightenment

The dynamic of faith is a mystery outside the scope of the historian, and it reaches far deeper than my feeble mind is willing to go. But one thing seems clear from this encounter on the Emmaus road. For these individuals at least, authentic belief is the culmination of a process, involving both the heart and the mind.

Their journey of faith begins in despair and disillusionment. It is kept alive by a passionate debate, with arguments and counter-arguments on both sides. It is interrupted—or so it seems—by the ignorance of a stranger. And then it is provoked by an uncompromising and probing look at the Word of God. Up until now, the Scripture has been a book of rituals, rules, warnings, and judgments. But somehow the stranger has illuminated it as if they were hearing it for the first time. "Is not my word like fire," God once declared to the Jews,"and like a hammer that breaks a rock in pieces?"[29]

The fire of faith has been lit in the hearts of these men. But it does not fan into flame until they reach their destination, the village of Emmaus.

It is almost evening as the disciples approach the village, and they persuade the stranger to come home with them and join them for a meal. What happens after they arrive involves a mysterious interaction between the natural and the supernatural: *"So he went in to stay with them. When he was at the table with them, he took bread, gave thanks, broke it and began to give it to them. Then their eyes were opened and they recognized him, and he disappeared from their sight."*

Students of the ancient world tell us that hospitality was a crucial feature of everyday life in the Israel of Jesus' day. It was, in fact, a matter of survival. There were no motel chains or fast-food outlets for weary travelers. People on a journey had to depend on the kindness of others for safety, lodging, and food. As one scholar described it, hospitality was considered "a pillar on which the moral structure of the world rested."[30] Without it, a simple trip to a neighboring city could become a tragedy of needless suffering.

Hospitality usually involved shared meals, which implied acceptance and fellowship. As a full-blooded Italian American, I can tell you that many of the richest and most intimate moments in life occur around the dinner table, with food and wine at the ready. When we sit down for a meal in the Loconte or Aiello families, we are never in a hurry; to wolf down a lovingly prepared plate of manicotti would be a crime against humanity. We gather not only for food, but to be together, to share a story and to hear what is on each other's hearts.

Jesus enjoyed many such moments with his followers, including our two travelers on the Emmaus road. Indeed, it says something about the importance of this custom—about the intimacy of a shared meal—that before his arrest and execution Jesus chose to enjoy a final meal with his closest friends. It is unclear whether Cleopas and his companion were present at that "last supper." But both were part of the inner circle of Jesus' followers and would have been with him many times when he paused to thank God, to break bread, and to pass around a cup of water or wine.

In the fellowship and vulnerability of a simple meal, something is revealed to us about the nature of faith. *"He took bread, gave thanks, broke it and began to give it to them. Then their eyes were opened and they recognized him."* What happens when we give thanks to God, not as a ritual, but out of humility and gratitude for his kindness to us?

Perhaps this is how the natural world is opened up to the supernatural. The homely experience of offering thanks to God and breaking bread together with Jesus helps to remove whatever obstacle was keeping these men from realizing who he was. Throughout their journey they have debated and inquired. With their intellect and their reason, they have sought to understand the death of Jesus and the identity of the Messiah. They have engaged with the Scripture and pondered its meaning.

Now, finally, their eyes are opened to the truth in front of them. Where there once was darkness, now there is light.

We think of the Age of Enlightenment as a time when people began to think for themselves and to throw off the shackles of religion and superstition, when "the lights began to come on in men's minds and humankind moved forward."[31] There was much about the Enlightenment quest that was impressive: its belief in reason, in natural rights, and in every person's obligation to pursue truth for themselves. Many Christian thinkers endorsed the Enlightenment defense of the rights of conscience. Eventually, however, religion was viewed as the friend of ignorance and the enemy of knowledge.

Yet the description of belief on the road to Emmaus—a pattern seen often in the Bible—suggests just the opposite. Christian faith, it turns out, involves the mind as well as the heart; reason as well as intuition. When these men shared a table with the stranger, their thoughts were drawn back to the many times they had done the same with Jesus: the teacher they had come to regard as the greatest prophet ever sent by God, a man to be followed, listened to, and obeyed at all costs.

Now, at this moment, they not only know the truth about Jesus. They are ready, fully ready, to *submit themselves to this truth*. Whatever it might mean, wherever it may lead them, they will act on the knowledge that has been revealed to them.

Faith and Freedom

Here is a glimpse into the nature of Christian conversion, an act of commitment that demands the whole man and the whole woman: heart, soul, and mind. Contrary to what is taught in some Christian churches, no one—not even God himself—will make this commitment for us. We must be persuaded of the truth about Jesus for ourselves, just as the two friends on the Emmaus road were guided out of their doubt and into belief. Authentic faith cannot be compelled; it cannot be imposed by fiat. Unlike most other belief systems in the world, Christian faith involves a relationship of trust—and no real relationship exists that has not been embraced freely in the heart and the mind.

Wherever we may be on our journey of faith, at least one threshold must be crossed. We must be willing to reconsider our assumptions about Jesus and the meaning of his life and ministry. Many people throughout history have claimed to discover Jesus "as he really was." Bookstores are littered with the latest "quest for the historical Jesus." Rebel, pacifist, socialist, moralist, fundamentalist, feminist, environmentalist—nearly everyone wants Jesus to endorse their partisan agenda. They seem less concerned with truth than with the success of their cause.

The questions before us about Jesus and his mission are the same ones that faced the disciples on the road to Emmaus. Are we willing to break with conventional wisdom? Do we love the truth more than we do our own ideas, traditions, and ambitions? Put simply, are we ready to confront the Jesus of the Bible—in his own words and on his own terms?

The philosopher Immanuel Kant, who could not accept the

Christian idea of God intruding into our earthly lives, praised the Enlightenment as "the emancipation of the human consciousness from an immature state of ignorance and error."[32] He was partly right. In Christian terms, true enlightenment does mean freedom—but it is freedom from the ego and selfishness and shame that has enslaved the souls of men and women from the dawn of civilization. "You will know the truth," Jesus promised his followers, "and the truth will set you free."[33]

Only an act of God's grace can offer this freedom, and only a willing and humble heart can accept it. Only then can enlightenment come: *"Then their eyes were opened and they recognized him."*

MYTH BECOMES FACT

"They got up and returned at once to Jerusalem. There they found the Eleven and those with them, assembled together and saying, 'It is true! The Lord has risen and has appeared to Simon.' Then the two told what had happened on the way, and how Jesus was recognized by them when he broke the bread."

———◆———

Nearly one hundred thousand hysterical fans, most of them women, have gathered outside the Frank E. Campbell Funeral Chapel in New York City to convince themselves that silent screen idol Rudolph Valentino is really dead. It all seems like a nightmare. In his breakout film, The Sheik, *Valentino invaded the imagination of millions of women with his dark Italian features, piercing eyes, and powerful and seductive persona. He instantly became for them "the Latin Lover," the romantic ideal. In a few short years he was the most fanatically adored movie star in history.*

Yet Valentino's playboy lifestyle caught up with him at a cocktail party, when he suddenly took ill and was rushed to a hospital. After a painful struggle, he succumbed to a perforated ulcer on August 23, 1926. The man who carried himself like one of the immortal gods was dead at the age of thirty-one. "While there have been many romantic leading men since Valentino," writes film historian James Steffen, "arguably none has had such a profound impact on American popular culture."[1]

Upon news of his death, two women killed themselves outside the hospital. Several others attempted suicide. In London, a girl swallowed poison in front of his photograph. Women everywhere, it seemed, were in mourning.

Now, at Valentino's funeral in New York, emotions are building to a new crescendo. Laid out in an open casket on a raised pedestal, Valentino is dressed in a dinner jacket and covered in heavy pancake makeup. His mouth, still twisted in pain, is cosmetically transformed into a seductive smile. A riot breaks out as fans jostle each other for a final glimpse. A spokesman for the funeral home summarizes the scene: "Never before have so many persons tried to see a body."[2]

After the funeral one of Valentino's ex-wives "refused to accept the idea he was dead" and claimed to communicate with him years after his death.[3] Many others did the same; the Valentino "death cult" emerged almost immediately after his passing. Books such as The Return of Rudolph Valentino *and* Rudolph Valentino Is My Spirit Friend *offer tales of psychic connections with the actor from beyond the grave. At the Hollywood Forever Cemetery, alleged sightings of Valentino continue to this day.*

Few personalities have generated such intense, otherworldly claims as Rudolph Valentino. As leading lady Alice Terry put it, "The biggest thing Valentino ever did was to die."[4]

There is a temptation to view the story of Jesus' death and resurrection in the same light as the carnival atmosphere surrounding the death of Rudolph Valentino. It certainly sounds like a familiar story: the career of an intensely popular and charismatic figure is cut tragically short—followed by tales from confused and overwrought women, denials that he is dead, rumors of shadowy appearances, and messages from beyond the grave. It is no surprise, we are told, that a post-mortem narrative for Jesus would be created. Sightings of a resurrected Messiah were as predictable as visions of Valentino's ghost.

But were they? When actually put to the test, this hasty judgment dissolves, like a snowflake into a furnace, as we consider again the events on the road to Emmaus.

We have already noted the gospel's insistence that the two disciples of Jesus *were kept from recognizing him* on their journey. If they are in a Valentino-like frame of mind, then why don't they instantly "realize" who this stranger is? Why the prolonged ignorance of his true identity? The account makes sense only if they are totally unprepared for the thought that the Teacher, brutalized and murdered by the Romans, might somehow overcome death.

As we'll explore in a moment, no one closely associated with Jesus suspects anything of the sort. There was no category in Jewish thought for the spontaneous bodily resurrection of a dead man. The end of Jesus meant the end of his mission. Period. As historian Paul Johnson observes, the Jesus movement instantly disintegrated after his execution: "It virtually ceased to exist."[5]

Something—something immensely powerful and attractive—brought the movement back into existence. What was it?

Historians of antiquity, secular and religious alike, agree on at least one fact: the followers of Jesus became convinced that they saw him alive after his crucifixion. According to Luke's account: *"They got up and returned at once to Jerusalem. There they found the Eleven and those with them, assembled together and saying, 'It is true! The Lord has risen and has appeared to Simon!'"*

It was this belief—not a new code of morality—that caused the Jesus movement to reemerge and reorganize itself. It was the proclamation of this event, an event they claimed to have witnessed, which mobilized his followers and made their influence felt throughout the Roman Empire. "The conviction that Jesus continued to live," writes philosopher Huston Smith, "transformed a dozen or so disconsolate followers of a slain and discredited leader into one of the most dynamic groups in human history."[6]

Highways to Heaven

All this might be true, but it still leaves many people wondering: Isn't belief in the resurrection of Jesus simply proof that his followers were products of a superstitious age? Given the plethora of ancient myths about gods who died and came back to life, what else would we expect?

There were, to be sure, no shortage of ancient cults that based their stories, rites, and symbols on gods and goddesses who enacted the natural cycle of the seasons, the pattern of death and rebirth. There were corn kings and corn mothers in abundance. There were deities such as Adonis, Attis, Demeter, Dionysus, Isis, and Osiris. The idea was to make contact with the supernatural forces that controlled the natural world, to win their cooperation, if not their love. For many ordinary people in the ancient Near East, the fertility of their crops—and the health of their tribe or nation—depended on these rituals and beliefs.

British scholar N. T. Wright explains that, by the time of the early Christians, just about everyone was familiar with these beliefs, thanks to migration and military conquests that carried them all over the Roman world. And, yes, at their heart was a powerful idea: "The myth which accompanied these rituals was indeed the story of resurrection, of new life on the other side of death."[7]

Thus the conclusion seems obvious: the first Christians hijacked this pagan myth to help them make sense of the death of Jesus. Anthropologist Joseph Campbell, for example, in a series of interviews with PBS personality Bill Moyers, argued exactly along these lines. In their conversations, later published as the bestselling *The Power of Myth*, Campbell accused the early Christians of confusing "misunderstood mythologies" with "hard fact." In other words, true believers mistakenly interpreted fables and fairytales as things that really happened.[8]

The big problem with this idea is that no worshipper at any time in any of these cults, from Egypt to northern Europe, thought that human beings, once dead, actually came back to life. All of their rituals enacting the death and resurrection of their gods were understood as a metaphor: they were symbols of the harvest or of human fertility. Nothing else. Occasionally, as in Egypt, the myth involved a funeral ritual in which the deceased might be united with Osiris in a murky underworld. But no one imagined a return trip to the life of the present world. "Nobody actually expected the mummies to get up, walk about and resume normal living," concludes N. T. Wright. "Nobody in that world would have wanted such a thing, either."[9]

The point must not be missed: the ancients shared a hope in life after death but not in the bodily resurrection of the dead in this life. No one believed that a corpse could rejoin the land of the living. *All the traffic on the highway to heaven moved in one direction.*[10]

Israel and the Shadow of Death

If this was what the ancients thought about death, what about the Jews? Didn't they already have a concept of resurrection by the time Jesus arrived on the scene? They did indeed—but not anything like the story offered to us in the encounter on the way to Emmaus.

There is a strong sense of hope among the Hebrew writers, even in the face of the grim certainty and finality of death. Usually this hope is applied to the nation of Israel as a community, that it would flourish and be restored to fellowship with God. At other times, though, the promise of life beyond the grave is held out to individuals, as well as to the nation.

"He will swallow up death forever," wrote Isaiah. "The Sovereign LORD will wipe away the tears from all faces."[11] King David was confident that God "will not abandon me to the realm of the dead," or let his soul vanish into eternal darkness. Rather, he said, "you will fill me with joy in your presence, with eternal pleasures at your right hand."[12] The prophet Daniel predicted the resurrection of both the righteous and the unrighteous: "Multitudes who sleep in the dust of the earth will awake: some to everlasting life, others to shame and everlasting contempt."[13]

Perhaps the most beautiful expression in the Bible of the hope of eternal life with God is found in Psalm 23:

> The LORD is my shepherd; I shall not want.
> He makes me to lie down in green pastures;
> He leads me beside the still waters.
> He restores my soul;
>> He leads me in paths of righteousness
>> For His name's sake.
> Yea, though I walk through the valley of the shadow of death,
>> I will fear no evil;
>> For You are with me;
>> Your rod and Your staff, they comfort me.
> You prepare a table before me in the presence of my enemies;
>> You anoint my head with oil;
>> My cup runs over.
> Surely goodness and mercy shall follow me
>> All the days of my life;
>> And I will dwell in the house of the LORD
>> Forever. (NKJV)

Thus, many Jews in Jesus' day believed in the physical resurrection of the body. They thought that those favored by God would somehow overcome the ravages of death and be reunited with him, body and soul. Yet they understood this as something that happened *at the end of time*, not in real time in their own day. Dead men stayed dead—at least for now. Nearly all the references to eternal life in the Old Testament were interpreted in this way.

The Jewish belief in resurrection, then, doesn't fit at all with the account of the two disciples on the Emmaus road. The emphasis in our story is on the actual, physical appearance of Jesus to his followers shortly after his death. It is set in the here and now, not in a distant, apocalyptic future.

The claim that a man known to be dead was seen alive would have been as incredible to the Jew as to the pagan. As scholar George Eldon Ladd concludes: "We have found nothing in either the Old Testament or contemporary Judaism to help us explain the rise of belief in the resurrection of Jesus."[14] This is why the discovery of an empty tomb—the failure to find the body of Jesus where it ought to have been—did not persuade his followers that he was alive. Something else must have convinced them.

Modern Myths and Harry Potter

Our account in Luke leaves no doubt about what that something was: Jesus has conquered death and appeared to his closest friends, to those in Jerusalem and to the two companions on the Emmaus road.

Before we unpack this claim, let's admit that the idea of resurrection is now firmly planted in the mind of the West, thanks to the success of the Christian story. It did not arrive from the Greeks, the Romans, or the mystery cults of the ancient world. It owes nothing to the Eastern concept of reincarnation. Even the Jews could not conceive of the dead reappearing in this life. Put simply, resurrection is a thoroughly Christian concept.

If the idea of resurrection seems ridiculous, we're left with the strange fact that the storytellers of our culture—the writers, artists, and filmmakers—can't help but appropriate it and make it a major theme of their work. I'm not thinking of marketing ploys, like Jean-Pierre Jeunet's *Alien Resurrection* (1997) or Lauren Lazin's 2003 documentary, *Tupac: Resurrection*, which uses dialogue from slain rapper Tupac Shakur to give the impression that he's speaking from the grave. Nor do I mean the latest raft of zombie books and films since, by definition, zombies are *the walking dead*.

I mean those artists whose work depends on the hope of resurrection. The most recent and best-known example is J. K. Rowling's *Harry Potter* series.[15] There are many reasons for the phenomenal success of these books (and the movies based upon them), which worldwide have sold more than 450 million copies in sixty-seven languages. The perennial appeal of witchcraft and wizardry, the magical beasts, the endless adventures and dangers, the bond of friendship between Harry Potter, Ron Weasley, and Hermione Granger—millions of young readers have found the stories impossible to resist.

Yet one of the major threads of Rowling's storytelling is the theme of death and rebirth. The series opens with the death of Harry's parents, murdered by the wicked Voldemort, the Dark Lord. There is the loss of friends and classmates in the struggle against him and his minions. There is, in fact, a shadow of death stalking Harry through the entire series. As Rowling puts it: "My books are largely about death."[16]

Rowling's books are not only about death, of course, but about the power of love to overcome death. In *The Sorcerer's Stone*, we learn that Harry's mother sacrificed her own life to rescue him and protect him from the deathgrip of Voldemort, his archenemy. In *Chamber of Secrets*, Harry is poisoned by the lethal venom of the King of Serpents. As he pulls the fang out of his arm, he hears the taunting voice of Riddle above him: "You're dead, Harry Potter." It looks as though he is—until he is saved by the healing tears of a phoenix, sent by the Great Wizard, the loving Dumbledore. In *Goblet of Fire*, Harry finds himself in a graveyard facing an almost certain death in a showdown with Voldemort. Only the assistance of his dead father, who appears to him in a spiritualized form, allows Harry to escape.

It is his obsession with cheating death that drives the Dark Lord in his pursuit of the Resurrection Stone. Voldemort will do anything, commit any atrocity, to possess it and restore his dissolved body to life. Thus the prophecy he seeks to fulfill: "The Dark Lord will rise again with his servant's aid, greater and more terrible than ever before." In the final book of the series, *Harry Potter and the Deathly Hallows*, Voldemort strikes down Harry with the Elder Wand, believing he can use Harry's blood to resurrect himself.

"I so understand why Voldemort wants to conquer death," says Rowling. "We're all frightened of it."[17] In *Harry Potter*, the remedy for this fear is sacrificial love: the giving of oneself in order to save another from great harm. Harry's blood carries the love of his mother for him—a love stronger than death—and it proves to be the ultimate power against Voldemort's wickedness.

Jesus, the Antidote to Death

In the *Harry Potter* phenomenon, then, we face this tantalizing truth: the most successful work of fiction in modern times draws its narrative strength from the Christian idea that sacrificial love—love unto death—can rescue people from the grip of evil, even from death itself.

No matter how we read the gospel stories, it's clear that many who knew Jesus—or knew something about him—believed he had the antidote to death. We see this in the encounter with Lazarus and his sisters, Martha and Mary. When Jesus arrived at the home of his stricken friend, already dead and buried, his sisters went to him and, with anguished hearts, exclaimed: "Lord, if you had been here, my brother would not have died."

Why would they think that Jesus had the power to hold back the shadow of death? Because they trusted him. They saw Jesus heal people on the edge of death. They heard him teach about the power of God to rescue his people from the darkest grave; they knew that this same power was alive in him. And they believed him. "I am the resurrection and the life," he told the sisters of Lazarus. "The one who believes in me will live, even though they die."[18] No rabbi, no guru, no leader of any pagan cult in the ancient world ever claimed such a thing. Yet Jesus immediately made good on his claim: he restored Lazarus to life.

We see this same confidence in Jesus expressed by the ruler of a synagogue, a man named Jairus, who came to him to plead for his daughter's life. "My little daughter is dying," he said. "Please come and put your hands on her so that she will be healed and live."[19] As far as this man was concerned, no doctor on earth could keep his daughter from the throes of death; Jesus was his only hope. Yet before Jesus could reach Jairus's house, the little girl succumbed. When he arrived, Jesus found a house full of mourners. "Why all this commotion and wailing?" he asked. "The child is not dead but asleep."[20]

A pleasant but meaningless metaphor? Here, instead, is a claim of such force that it threatens to scatter all rival beliefs like dust: as long as Jesus is present, the terror of death is no terror at all. *To Jesus the Rescuer, death is like a light sleep.* And so he reached down deep into death, took the little girl by the hand, and brought her back to life.[21]

Bearing Witness

When the two disciples realize who has been walking and talking with them on their journey, everything becomes shockingly clear. All their lives they have been mistaken about the Messiah, about his mission, and about the history of Israel. Their identity as Jews—as members of a "chosen nation"—has kept them from confronting their broken identities before God. They have allowed their dreams of political liberation to obscure their deepest moral and spiritual needs.

Now, finally, they understand what God has been doing in their world. The message from Jesus on the road to Emmaus is the same message that Christians have proclaimed for twenty centuries. It is that God sent his Son to rescue people from the curse of sin and death. It is the news that this Rescuer, Jesus, gave his life in exchange for ours—and then rose from the dead to offer us new life, an incorruptible life, with God. *It was love that sent the Rescuer to his death and love that raised him to life again.*

They must tell their friends what has happened! Cleopas and his companion rush back to Jerusalem, to the house where Jesus shared a last meal with his friends. There they find the inner circle of his followers, the men known as apostles, along with other followers and friends: *"There they found the Eleven and those with them, assembled together and saying, 'It is true! The Lord has risen and has appeared to Simon!'"* In a few breathless moments they learn that Jesus has appeared to his disciples in Jerusalem, just as he appeared to them on the Emmaus road. The women had been right all along: the tomb of Jesus was empty because he no longer belonged to the dead.

We're told that Jesus has also appeared to Simon, otherwise known as Peter, a fact that could be appreciated only by a handful of the disciples. Why mention it? Why is Peter singled out? Probably because it was Peter who, at the trial of Jesus, pretended not to know who he was. He was afraid of being exposed and arrested, and his fear led him to deny—emphatically, three times—that he had anything to do with Jesus.

If there is one experience that can break and debilitate a man, it is the experience of cowardice. To fail to do one's duty because of fear, to shrink back from conflict, to betray one's comrades in battle, to flee—the memory of cowardice can paralyze a man as surely as polio. Apart from Judas, who actually betrayed Jesus to the authorities, none of his friends failed him as conspicuously as Peter. The apostle must have felt utterly adrift. He had sworn loyalty no matter what the cost, but within moments of Jesus' arrest, he melted away in fear.

"When something like this happens you are lost," says Harry Faversham, the nineteenth-century British officer in A. E. W. Mason's novel *The Four Feathers*. Faversham had quit his military commission because of his fear of combat, only to receive a white feather from each of his closest friends. It was the symbol of disgrace. "You don't know who you are anymore and what you're capable of. Unless I do something, this is always how people will remember me. A feather. And that is how I will always see myself: a coward."[22]

Peter could easily have sunk into a mire of self-loathing for the rest of his days. He did not, and there is only one conceivable reason he did not: *"The Lord has risen and has appeared to Simon!"* Jesus sought out his friend to make things right. We do not know the content of their meeting, but we can be sure that Peter—who went on to proclaim the Christian message with great courage—found compassion and forgiveness.

And so we have another detail in Luke's narrative, a reconciliation, which rings true to human psychology. It fits with what we know about people in a crisis. It is a detail that is completely unnecessary, yet its inclusion reminds us of the rugged realism of the Bible and its intimate knowledge of our emotional, moral, and spiritual needs.

Why is all this important? Because it drives home the most controversial fact about the early Christian community: its basic message was not about morality but about a moment in time.

Within weeks of his death, the followers of Jesus appeared in public—in the streets and synagogues of Jerusalem—and insisted that he was alive. Despite intense hostility, they pressed home this claim again and again. Their emphasis was not on the ministry of Jesus, not on his teachings, not even on his sacrificial death. The heart of their "good news" was that Jesus had overcome death. "You killed the author of life," Peter told a crowd in Jerusalem, "but God raised him from the dead. We are witnesses of this."[23]

When we think of the early Christians, we remember their heart for the poor and marginalized in Roman society, their ethic of love of neighbor. But it was not their proclamation of the "golden rule" that got them into so much trouble. Christians weren't dragged into the Coliseum and fed to the lions because they were caught feeding the hungry. They were bullied and persecuted because they claimed to be witnesses: *they claimed to have seen something that had never been seen before in the history of the world.*

The Last Enemy

Earlier we learned that the idea of the resurrection of Jesus was unique in its day. It could not have been imagined by the ancient pagan religions, by the Greeks, or even by the Jews. In another sense, however, the Christian story of resurrection is a myth as old as civilization itself. It is hinted at in the rhythm of the natural world, and dimly understood by the philosophies and religions of the ancient world: death and rebirth.[24]

In the myths of Osiris and Dionysus, we read of gods who die only in the imagination; no one knows when or where they do their bit. But in the story about Jesus, we have a concrete, historical person who is executed under the political authority of an actual pagan ruler, Pontius Pilate. His death occurs in a real city, Jerusalem, in a public spectacle witnessed by his closest friends. We know this not only from the gospels, but also from accounts recorded by Roman and Jewish authors of the day.[25]

History cannot prove the resurrection story, but the facts of history lend weight to the declaration that Jesus rose from the dead—a claim that could not have been maintained for a single day in Jerusalem if his putrefying corpse was easily available for inspection. Other Jewish leaders and self-styled messiahs had come and gone, but no one ever suggested that they had come back to life; everyone knew where their bodies were buried. Something very different occurred in the case of Jesus.

"The heart of Christianity is a myth which is also a fact," wrote C. S. Lewis. "The old myth of the Dying God . . . comes down from the heaven of legend and imagination to the earth of history."[26] In the Christian story, myth becomes fact.

If so, it is a fact anticipated both by nature and human culture, especially the culture of the Jews. To the Jews of Jesus' day, death was an ongoing assault on the human race, a race of men and women made in the image of their Creator. Death was therefore an adversary, a force opposed to God, to his creation, and to his creatures. To the Jews, death was "the ultimate weapon of destruction."[27] The promised Messiah—if he were truly sent and empowered by God—would be the one to bring death to its knees. In the process, he would bring the kingdom of God into the hearts of men.

Thus in the person of Jesus we find not another moralist or social revolutionary or holy crusader. Rather, we encounter a man who seems to have the cure for humanity's "sickness unto death." Jesus himself once described his followers as "children of the resurrection."[28] As historian C. F. Evans summarized it, the religion of Jesus is "a religion of resurrection."

Perhaps this is why the hope of resurrection retains such a powerful appeal in our culture. In *Harry Potter and the Deathly Hallows*, Harry and his friends must dig deeply into the past to find the key to destroying Lord Voldemort, the embodiment of death itself. In his quest, Harry returns to the place of his birth—Godric's Hollow—where his parents gave their lives to save him. He visits the graveyard where they are buried. The words on their tombstone, taken almost verbatim from the New

Testament, are these: "The last enemy that shall be destroyed is death."[29]

The meaning of the resurrection of Jesus, the Easter story, is that this fearsome enemy has been vanquished by God himself. Life with God, eternal life, is now possible for those who seek it.

Two friends on a lonely road that leads to a small village called Emmaus have come to believe this story. Their hearts have been shaken loose from unbelief, their minds opened to truth and grace. They have learned the secret of the divine conspiracy, God's plan to use death against itself, to swallow up death by an indestructible Life. These followers of Jesus, joined by many others, cannot help but share this knowledge with everyone they meet, wherever they find themselves.

And the world, a world weary with beliefs that bring no lasting comfort, cannot help but stand up and take notice.

CONCLUSION

The Road Home

Art historians have observed that of all the painters of the early modern era, Rembrandt stands apart as one who sought to understand the encounter between the natural and the supernatural. Other artists drew from the Bible for their subjects, but their renderings often display a lofty spirituality: saintly figures that seem wholly disconnected from earthly life. For these painters, sinners and saints are easily distinguished.

Not for Rembrandt. Although a believing Christian and a keen student of the Bible, Rembrandt was not interested in debates over doctrine or the fine points of Christian morality. That probably had something to do with the era in which he worked. The first half of the seventeenth century in Europe was a season of religious conflict and persecution. Even Rembrandt's native Holland, a Protestant state more tolerant of religious differences than its European neighbors, struggled with militant Christianity. He could not have failed to observe the poison of religion: the cultural hatreds, under the banner of faith, that were directed against Protestant dissenters, Catholics, and Jews.

For whatever reason, Rembrandt was drawn to stories of the sinner who repents, of the wayward soul who receives forgiveness. No other artist of his day entered so sympathetically into the lives of his earthly subjects. "What he was really grappling with here," writes Greg Watts, "was the idea of God's grace, or power to transform and save a person."[1]

Rembrandt captures this concept in his magnificent 1644 painting *Christ and the Woman Taken in Adultery*. It tells the story of a woman, caught in adultery, brought before Jesus by the religious establishment. The authorities want her stoned to death, and press Jesus to approve their judgment. But he won't be lured into their trap: "Let any one of you who is without sin be the first to throw a stone at her."[2] One by one the accusers drift off in quiet embarrassment; no one comes forward to cast a stone. "Has no one condemned you?" he asks the woman. "Then neither do I condemn you. Go now and leave your life of sin."[3]

In Rembrandt's rendering, the woman kneels before Jesus, sorrowful, wearing a white garment. She seems to be illuminated by Jesus himself, who is dressed simply yet radiates warmth and compassion. The Scribes and Pharisees, by contrast, are dressed in elaborate costumes and hats, partially hidden in the shadows. The fact that their clothing is taken from Rembrandt's day suggests that the problem of hypocrisy in religion is ever with us.

For believers such as Rembrandt, the grace of God is always nearer to us than we think: the least "religious" people in the room are often closest to redemption. This may explain the artist's lifelong interest in the story of two friends, a stranger, and a conversation on the road to Emmaus. Rembrandt was drawn to this biblical scene again and again in his work; he was fascinated by the awakening of faith and hope in ordinary people.

As we have seen, the quickening of belief in the disciples was a process. They began their journey in a state of bewilderment and doubt, even despair. Their doctrines had let them down. Their religious leaders had misled them. God himself, it seemed, had turned his back on them. They were about as far from belief in the Messiah as any idol worshipper in Rome.

"If you would be a real seeker after truth," wrote French philosopher Rene Descartes, "it is necessary that at least once in your life you doubt, as far as possible, all things." Whatever we might think of that skeptical advice, it's a good bet that it describes the outlook of the disciples for much of their journey.

Nevertheless, their doubts collide with reality on the way to Emmaus. They are dragged into the realm of truth and grace by the presence of Jesus.

And, yet, his presence at first almost offends us. He does not hesitate to rebuke the travelers for their lack of faith, chiding them as "foolish" and "slow to believe." The problem hindering these men was not a deficit of facts or evidence for belief. It was an unwillingness to think differently, to give up their false assumptions, to admit that they might be terribly wrong about God.

There is a mystery here we cannot fully grasp, the movement of a human soul from skepticism to faith.

One thing we must not do is use the mystery of belief as a reason to delay a judgment about belief. The idea of remaining neutral or agnostic about religious questions is in vogue today. No one wants to be accused of being dogmatic or, God forbid, a fundamentalist. Thus, there are many people who describe themselves as "spiritual but not religious." Others even boast about their "epistemological humility," that is, their shyness about agreeing that anything can be known about God or his purpose for our lives. These strategies usually amount to the same thing: an evasion of responsibility.

Even historians who emphasize the limits of history in probing this mystery admit the implications of the account that has come down to us. The story of the death and resurrection of Jesus "cannot be left merely to the philosopher or to the poet as though it were a contribution to speculation or to culture," according to British scholars Sir Edwyn Hoskyns and Noel Davey. "It records historical facts which demand the consideration and judgment of every man and woman."[4]

The claims of Jesus about his identity and mission do not allow for polite indifference. Why? Because we are being asked to make a decision.

If the Christian story is true, then human life has a meaning and a destination. Its purpose is concentrated in a single individual, acting in a definite moment in time. His triumph over evil and death is the focal point of world history. Even more, his victory signals *the end of history*, the beginning of the end of a world in the grip of spiritual slavery. "They will know that I am the Lord," God promised his people, "when I break the bars of their yoke and rescue them from the hands of those who enslaved them."[5]

The Rescuer, Jesus, has come to set us free. The captives now have a choice: to leave with him, to go to our true home and live in freedom, or to bid him goodbye and remain where we are and suffer in bondage. There is no middle ground. C. S. Lewis addressed this theme when he compared the arrival of God on earth, at the end of time, to an author who walks on stage when the play he has written is over:

> God is going to invade, all right: but what is the good of saying
> you are on his side then, when you see the whole natural universe

melting away like a dream and something else—something it
never entered your head to conceive—comes crashing in; something so beautiful to some of us and so terrible to others that
none of us will have any choice left? For this time it will be God
without disguise; something so overwhelming that it will strike
either irresistible love or irresistible horror into every creature. It
will be too late then to choose your side.[6]

We have seen how two companions, on their way to a place
called Emmaus, were confronted with a similar choice. They
were not expecting to meet with God as they fled the scene
where their hopes had collapsed into futility. They had set their
sights on home, where they might make sense of things. Home
would be a place of escape.

What they finally realized was that God had a much better home for them in mind: a new heaven and a new earth.
It is a place where longings are fulfilled and sorrows forgotten,
where joy runs like a mighty river through every human heart.
Here our incurable wound is finally healed. In this new home
we see the face of the hidden God, and we walk with him as a
man walks with his friend. "My Father's house has many rooms,"
Jesus told his followers. "I am going there to prepare a place for
you. And if I go and prepare a place for you, I will come back
and take you to be with me."[7]

We may choose life in this home with God—or not. His
offer of freedom and forgiveness extends to everyone—to all
those "living in darkness and in the shadow of death"—and his
grace stands ready to help us in our choice.[8] As Jesus did with
the travelers on the Emmaus road, God is holding back to give
each of us a chance.

Yet we cannot keep our options open forever. When our minds are not muddled by distractions, we know this to be true.

Remember the character of Treebeard, a leader among the race of Ents, the shepherds of the forest in *The Lord of the Rings*? The Ents are described as a "deliberate" people, extremely slow to decide on a course of action. In reality, they are eager to avoid committing themselves in the great contest against the Dark Lord. "I am not altogether on anybody's side," Treebeard explains, "because nobody is altogether on my side."[9] Up until the eleventh hour, the Ents hope to maintain a policy of strict neutrality. But their desire to be left alone—their refusal to choose Goodness—becomes untenable as the dark forces of Mordor gather against the inhabitants of Middle-earth:

> "Of course, it is likely enough, my friends," Treebeard said slowly, "likely enough that we are going to our doom: the last march of the Ents. But if we stayed at home and did nothing, doom would find us anyway, sooner or later. That thought has long been growing in our hearts; and that is why we are marching now."[10]

Wherever we are in our journey, whatever we believe, our earthly march will come to an end. Whether we meet Jesus at the moment of our death, or when he comes again—without disguise—we will face him. With heads bowed, either in love or grief, we will face him. For he has promised to return, in the fullness of time, to cast off the faithless, but to rescue all those who wish to be free.

"That will not be the time for choosing," warns Lewis. "It will be the time when we discover which side we really have chosen, whether we realized it or not."[11]

Acknowledgments

There are many, many people whose love, friendship, and wisdom have been great gifts to me over the years and who have contributed, directly and indirectly, to the strengths of the book (I take full responsibility for its weaknesses). They include Suzanne and Joe Middleton, Mike and Ann Marie Loconte, and my extended Italian family; friends Ken and Marilyn Jackson, Mark and Patti Kreslins, Kara Callaghan, Cherie Harder, Eric Metaxas, Lia and Charles Howard, Jedd and Rachel Medefind, Ed and Karen Moy, Kevin and Amy Offner, Charlie Catlett, Tim Schwartz, Fred Ferrara, Pete Peterson, Tim Montgomerie, Benedict Rogers, Daniel Johnson, Chuck Colson, Marvin Olasky, Russ Pulliam, Michael Cromartie, and Os Guinness.

I want to thank my literary agent, Joel Kneedler at Alive Communications, for his great encouragement in pursuing the book idea, and his steady support throughout the process. I am deeply grateful to Joel Miller, vice president of editorial and acquisitions at Thomas Nelson, for his faith in the project, and to editor Janene MacIvor for her great skill and patience in guiding the editorial process along.

Tessa Carter, a student of mine at the King's College, served as my research assistant and made an outstanding contribution. Tessa's knowledge of literature and film, a treasure trove of wisdom, enriched the book enormously. Special thanks also belong to Lia Howard, a Critical Writing Fellow at the University of Pennsylvania. With her relentless enthusiasm and literary savvy, Lia read over the entire manuscript and made numerous suggestions and improvements. Her editorial and conceptual insights were indispensable, and strengthened the book in countless ways.

I also want to thank my students and colleagues at the King's College in New York City for all their support, encouragement, and solidarity in the journey of faith.

Notes

Introduction: Two Friends on a Quest

1. The Jesus movement, of which these men were a part, was thrown into crisis upon his death. Because the Romans executed Jesus on the charge of sedition, it was not safe for his followers to remain in Jerusalem. Although scholars debate the actual location of Emmaus, Luke identifies it as a village seven miles from the city. It seems reasonable to infer that these disciples lived in Emmaus, and were returning there to find refuge. See, for example, N. T. Wright, *The Resurrection of the Son of God* (Minneapolis: Fortress Press, 2003), 647–661; Joel B. Green, *The Gospel of Luke* (Grand Rapids: Eerdmans, 1997), 840–859; and F. F. Bruce, *New Testament History* (Garden City: Doubleday, 1980), 195–204.

2. The Greek word to describe their conversation, *syzetein*, suggests an intense debate. Darrell L. Bock, *Luke: The NIV Application Commentary* (Grand Rapids: Zondervan, 1996), 612.

3. George S. Keyes, "Perception and Belief," *Rembrandt and the Face of Jesus* (Philadelphia: Philadelphia Museum of Art, 2011), 22.

4. Jaroslav Pelikan, *Jesus Through the Centuries: His Place in the History of Culture* (New Haven: Yale Univ. Press, 1985), 1.

5. Jesus was arrested by Jewish temple guards and servants of the Jewish High Priest because of his religious claims. But he soon was turned over to the Romans to be executed on political charges, including the fomenting of insurrection. See Bruce M. Metzger, *The New Testament: Its Background, Growth and Content* (Nashville: Abingdon Press, 1991), 122–124.

6. Martin Goodman, *Rome and Jerusalem: The Clash of Ancient Civilizations* (New York: Vintage Books, 2007), 63–114.

7. Martin Hengel, *Crucifixion* (Philadelphia: Fortress Press, 1988), 22–25.

8. John 19:12.

9. Walker Percy, *The Moviegoer* (New York: Vintage International, 1998), 13.

10. J. R. R. Tolkien, *The Fellowship of the Ring* (Boston: Houghton Mifflin Company, 1994), 159.

11. Biblical scholars disagree about the identities of Cleopas and his companion. The former may be the "Clopas" mentioned in John 19:25, making him the husband of Mary, one of the women mentioned at the scene of the crucifixion. Some thus believe that the unnamed disciple was the wife of Cleopas. Others speculate that the latter disciple was Luke, the author of the gospel that bears his name. My own sense is that the unnamed disciple was a close friend or relative of Cleopas who preferred to keep his identity hidden.

12. Michael Wilcock, *The Message of Luke* (Downers Grove: InterVarsity Press, 1979), 18.

13. Marcus Aurelius, *Meditations* (New York: Alfred A. Knopf, 1992), 18–19.

14. Harold M. Schulweis, *For Those Who Can't Believe: Overcoming the Obstacles to Faith* (New York: HarperCollins Publishers, 1994), 2.

15. Percy, *The Moviegoer*, 11.

Chapter One: Things Seen and Unseen

1. Geoffrey Chaucer, *The Canterbury Tales*, translated by Christopher Lauer (New York: Bantam Dell, 2006), 14.

2. Paul Johnson, *A History of Christianity* (New York: Penguin Books, 1976), 267.

3. Quoted in "The Cult of 'St. Elvis,'" *Vision*, summer 2002.

4. Quotation #30163 from Michael Moncur's (Cynical) Quotations, The Quotations Page, accessed February 21, 2012, http://www.quotationspage.com/quote/30163.html.

5. Huston Smith, *The World's Religions* (New York: HarperCollins Publishers, 1991), 2.

6. Lynn Hunt, Thomas R. Martin, et. al., *The Making of the West: Peoples and Cultures* (Boston: Bedford/St. Martin's, 2011), 19.

7. Virgil, *The Aeneid*, translated by Robert Fagles (New York: Penguin Books, 2006), 141.

8. Leon R. Kass, *The Beginning of Wisdom: Reading Genesis* (New York: Free Press), 43.

9. Paul Johnson, *A History of the Jews* (New York: Harper & Row Publishers, 1987), 30.

10. Lam. 3:44.

11. Richard Tarnas, *The Passion of the Western Mind* (New York: Ballantine, 1991), 300.

12. Mitch Stokes, *Isaac Newton* (Nashville: Thomas Nelson, 2010), 83.

13. William Sweet and Richard Feist, eds., *Religion and the Challenges of Science* (Burlington: Ashgate, 2007), 41.

14. Peter Gay, *The Enlightenment: An Interpretation* (New York: W. W. Norton, 1995), 145.

15. Walter Isaacson, *Einstein: His Life and Universe* (New York: Simon and Schuster, 2007), 386.

16. John D. Barrow and Frank Tipler, *The Anthropic Cosmological Principle* (New York: Oxford Univ. Press, 1988), vii.

17. Fred Hoyle, "The Universe: Past and Present Reflections," *Engineering and Science*, November 1981, p. 12.

18. Richard Dawkins, *Blind Watchmaker* (New York: W. W. Norton, 1996), ix.

19. Mary Lea Bandy and Antonio Monda, *The Hidden God: Film and Faith* (New York: The Museum of Modern Art, 2003), 12.

20. *The Cloud of Unknowing* is a work of Christian mysticism, written anonymously in the 14th century.

21. Jaroslav Pelikan, ed., *Luther's Works*, vol. 54 (St. Louis: Concordia, 1986), 35.

22. G. S. Viereck, "What Life Means to Einstein," *Saturday Evening Post*, 26 October 1929.

23. Ezek. 34:11–12, 16.

24. John 10:11.

25. David Wenham, *The Parables of Jesus* (Downers Grove: InterVarsity Press, 1989), 102.

26. Luke 15:10.

27. Edward Buscombe, *The Searchers* (London: British Film Institute, 2011), 67.

28. Roger Ebert, *The Great Movies II* (New York: Broadway Books, 2005), 406.

29. George Eldon Ladd, *A Theology of the New Testament* (Grand Rapids: Eerdmans, 1994), 80.

30. Tarnas, *The Passion of the Western Mind*, 301.

31. Timothy Ferris, *The Whole Shebang: A State-of-the-Universe(s) Report* (New York: Touchstone, 1997), 312.

32. Ps. 139:1, 7–10.

33. Deut. 4:29.

34. Jer. 29:13.

35. 2 Chron. 7:14.

36. Ps. 9:10.

37. Abraham Joshua Heschel, *God in Search of Man: A Philosophy of Judaism* (New York: Farrar, Straus and Giroux, 1983), 85.

38. Blaise Pascal, *Pensees*, translated by William Finlayson Trotter, (London: Penguin Books, 1995), 142.

Chapter Two: A Grief Observed

1. Eric Metaxas, *Amazing Grace: William Wilberforce and the Heroic Campaign to End Slavery* (New York: HarperOne, 2007), 225.

2. Olaudah Equiano, *The Interesting Narrative of the Life of Olaudah Equiano*, Robert J. Allison, ed. (Boston: Bedford/St. Martin's, 2007), 58–69.

3. Homer, *The Illiad*, translated by Samuel Butler, book 24, http://classics.mit.edu/Homer/iliad.mb.txt.

4. Joan Didion, *The Year of Magical Thinking* (New York: Vintage International, 2005), 35.

5. Ibid., 37.

6. John 19:34.

7. Rex W. Huppke, "Four Deaths in Freak Accident Test a Congregation," *The Washington Post*, January 6, 2002, A10.

8. Rashid Razaq, Peter Dominiczak, and Benedict-Moore Bridger, "Japan Earthquake Survivor: 'There Was a Silence Like the World Had Stopped . . . Then the Quake Hit,'" *The London Evening Standard*, March 11, 2011.

9. The quote comes from a live report from CNN broadcast the week following the tsunami.

10. Mohamed Sheikh Nor and Jason Straziuso, "Famine's Devastation: Four Dead Children, One Family," *Orange County Register*, Aug. 8, 2011.

11. Nazila Fathi, "In a Death Seen Round the World, A Symbol of Iranian Protests," *The New York Times*, June 22, 2009.

12. Joseph Loconte, "Nearer, My God to the G.O.P.," *The New York Times*, January 2, 2006.

13. C. S. Lewis, *A Grief Observed* (New York: Bantam Books, 1976), 1–39.

14. Ibid., 5.

15. *Gilgamesh*, translated by Stephen Mitchell (New York: Free Press, 2004), 1.

16. Ibid., 145.

17. Ibid.

18. Ibid., 153.

19. Ibid., 152–153.

20. Smith, *The World's Religions*, 84.

21. Ibid., 82–149.

22. Jeremy Brett, who played Holmes in the Granada TV adaptation of "The Adventure of the Cardboard Box," delivered these lines at the end of the television series, which follow closely Doyle's text.

23. Lam. 1:16.

24. Matt. 2:16.

25. Matt. 2:18.

26. Matt. 8:1–4; Mark 1:40–45; Luke 5:12–14.

27. Luke 5:12.

28. Ibid.

29. Luke 5:13.

30. I am indebted to the public lectures and writings of Os Guinness on this topic. See Os Guinness, *Unspeakable: Facing Up to Evil in an Age of Genocide and Terror* (New York: HarperCollins, 2005), 143–145.

31. John 11:34–35.

32. Luke 8:13.

33. Cormac McCarthy, *The Road* (New York: Vintage International, 2006), 14.

34. Ibid., 129–30.

35. Thucydides, *The Peloponnesian War*, translated by Martin Hammond (Oxford: Oxford Univ. Press, 2009), 99.

36. *Faith and Doubt at Ground Zero*, PBS documentary.

37. *Gilgamesh*, 159.

38. Lance Morrow, *Evil: An Investigation* (New York: Basic Books, 2003), 108.

39. C. S. Lewis, *A Grief Observed*, 61.

40. Roland H. Bainton, *Here I Stand: A Life of Martin Luther* (New York: Mentor Books, 1977), 237.

Chapter Three: The Poison of Religion

1. Hans R. Guggisberg, *Sebastian Castellio, 1515–1563* (Burlington: Ashgate, 2003), 79.
2. Juan Naya and Marian Hillar, *Michael Servetus, Heartfelt: Proceedings of the International Servetus Congress*, Barcelona, October 20-21, 2006, xvi.
3. *Pascal: Pensees*, 265.
4. W. E. Vine, *Expository Dictionary of New Testament Words* (Grand Rapids, Zondervan, 1952), 222.
5. Matt. 5:3.
6. John 5:8.
7. Matt. 27:18.
8. Matt. 12:34, 23:27; Luke 11:44; 1 John 3:10.
9. David L. Goetz, *Death by Suburb: How to Keep the Suburbs from Killing Your Soul* (New York: HarperCollins, 2006), 9.
10. Ben Conery, "Supreme Court Hears Arguments on Church Protests at Military Funerals," *The Washington Times*, Oct. 6, 2010.
11. Patsy McGarry, "Commission Finds Church Covered Up Sex Abuse," *Irish Times*, Nov. 26, 2009.
12. Michael E. Ruane and William Wan, "Vatican Priest Likens Criticism of Church on Abuse to Anti-Semitism," *The Washington Post*, April 3, 2010.
13. C. S. Lewis, *The Four Loves* (San Diego: Harcourt Brace Jovanovich, 1988), 49.
14. Desiderius Erasmus, *The Praise of Folly* (New York: W. W. Norton, 1989), 97.
15. The History Channel (1999), *The Inquisition*.
16. Michael C. Thomsett, *The Inquisition: A History* (Jefferson, NC: McFarland, 2010), 158.
17. Johnson, *A History of Christianity*, 298–99.
18. Ibid., 308.
19. John Olin, ed., *Christian Humanism and the Reformation: Selected Writings of Erasmus* (New York: Fordham Univ. Press, 1987), 195.
20. Philip van Limborch, *The History of the Inquisition* (London, 1731), 124–125; 17.

21. John Coffey, *Persecution and Toleration in Protestant England* (Harlow: Pearson Education Ltd., 2000), 166.

22. John Tillotson, "Of Sincerity Towards God and Man," Sermon the First. Preach'd at Kingston, July 29, 1694, London: 1735, 11–12.

23. John Norton and Susan Mendus, eds., *John Locke: A Letter Concerning Toleration in Focus* (London: Routledge, 2004), 38.

24. Luke 12:1.

25. Meris Lutz, "Babylon and Beyond," *Los Angeles Times*, February 12, 2010.

26. Ayaan Hirsi Ali, *Infidel* (New York: Free Press, 2007), 230.

27. "Pakistani Lawmaker Defends Honor Killings," Associated Press, August 30, 2008.

28. Dan Bilefsky, "How to Avoid Honor Killing in Turkey? Honor Suicide," *The New York Times*, July 16, 2006.

29. *9/11 Commission Report: Final Report of the National Commission of Terrorist Attacks Upon the United States* (Washington, D.C.: U.S. Government Printing Office, 2004), 48.

30. Scot Shifrel and Larry Mcshane, "Defiant Faisal Shahzad, Pakistani Immigrant Who Tried to Bomb Times Square, Sentenced to Life," *Daily News*, October 5, 2010.

31. Bernard Lewis, "What Went Wrong?" *The Atlantic Monthly*, January 2002.

32. Barbara *Kingsolver, The Poisonwood Bible* (New York: HarperCollins, 2002), 96.

33. Christopher Hitchens, *God is Not Great: How Religion Poisons Everything* (New York: Hatchet Book Group USA, 2007), 8.

34. Frederick M. Shepherd, *Christianity and Human Rights: Christians and the Struggle for Global Justice* (Lanham: Lexington Books, 2009), 67.

35. Sebastian Castellio, *Concerning Heretics* (New York: Octagon Books, 1979), 125.

36. Norton and Mendus, eds., *John Locke*, 14.

37. William Hague, *William Wilberforce: The Life of the Great Anti-Slave Trade Campaigner* (London: HarperCollins, 2007), 179.

38. Eric Metaxas, *Bonhoeffer: Pastor, Martyr, Prophet, Spy* (Nashville: Thomas Nelson, 2011), 154.

39. William James, *The Varieties of Religious Experience* (New York: Penguin Books, 1985), 259–260.

40. Ibid., 357–358.
41. Matt. 9:12–13.
42. Luke 7:49.
43. Luke 7:41–43.
44. Heschel, *God in Search of Man*, 10–11.
45. Jill Sherman, *The Hindenburg Disaster* (Minneapolis: ABDO Pub., 2010), 52.
46. Luke 7:44–47.
47. Thomas Paine, "The American Crisis," in *Paine: Collected Writings* (New York: Library of America, 1995), 92.

Chapter Four: The End of Illusions

1. Jon Krakauer, *Into the Wild*, author's note (New York: Anchor Books, 1997).
2. Ibid., 6.
3. Accessed March 19, 2012, http://www.worldofquotes.com/author/Henrik+Ibsen/1/index.html.
4. Mark 15:31.
5. *The Epic of Gilgamesh*, translated by Nancy K. Sandars (London: Penguin Books, 1972), 39.
6. Thomas More, *Utopia* (London: Penguin Books, 1965), 128.
7. Sigmund Freud, *The Future of an Illusion* (New York: W. W. Norton, 1975), 55–56.
8. Sam Harris, *The End of Faith: Religion, Terror, and the Future of Reason* (New York: W. W. Norton, 2004), 72.
9. Cheryl Lodico, *Robert Browning: Idealism and Disillusionment in His Life and Work* (Pittsburgh: Red Lead Press, 2007), 2.
10. Aviva Patz, "Will Your Marriage Last?" *Psychology Today*, January 1, 2000.
11. Stanlye H. Teitelbaum, *Illusion and Disullusionment: Core Issues in Psychotherapy* (Northvale: Jason Aronson, Inc., 1999), 28–29.
12. Virgil, *The Aeneid*, 140–141.
13. Whittaker Chambers, *Witness* (Washington, DC: Regnery, 1980), 9.
14. Ibid., 19–22.
15. Here I am speculating about the frame of mind of the disciples when they first encountered Jesus and his teaching. Nevertheless,

given the fact that false messiahs had come and gone in the years leading up to Jesus' ministry, it's a reasonable guess that Cleopas and his companion had to be persuaded to put their trust in him.

16. *The Killing Fields*, PBS documentary.
17. Barbara Tuchman, *The Guns of August* (New York: Ballantine Books, 1994), 141.
18. Winston S. Churchill, *Memoirs of the Second World War: An Abridgement of the Six Volumes of The Second World War* (Boston: Houghton Mifflin, 1987), 3.
19. Ray Abrams, *Preachers Present Arms* (New York: Round Table Press, 1933), 57.
20. Tuchman, *The Guns of August*, 523.
21. Erich Maria Remarque, *All Quiet on the Western Front* (New York: Fawcett, 1982), 79.
22. Bernard Lewis, *What Went Wrong? The Clash Between Islam and Modernity in the Middle East*, (New York: Perennial, 2002), 11.
23. Margaret MacMillan, *Paris 1919: Six Months That Changed the World* (New York: Random House, 2003), 369.
24. Mary Habeck, *Knowing the Enemy: Jihadist Ideology and the War on Terror* (New Haven: Yale Univ. Press, 2006), 26.
25. Bernard Lewis, *What Went Wrong?*, 43.
26. John Goldingay, *Key Questions About Christian Faith: Old Testatment Answers* (Grand Rapids, Baker, 2010), 109–110.
27. Lam. 1:2, 4.
28. Isa. 14:1–2.
29. Jer. 30:15–17.
30. 2 Sam. 7:12–14.
31. Zech. 9:9–10.
32. Isa. 9:6–7.
33. George Eldon Ladd, *The New Testament and Criticism* (Grand Rapids: Eerdmans, 1983), 174.
34. Luke 13:34.
35. Stephen Holden, "Johnny Cash, Country Music's Bare-Bones Realist, Dies at 71," *The New York Times*, September 12, 2003.
36. Chris Wrigley, *Winston Churchill: A Biographical Companion* (Santa Barbara: American Biographical Companions, 2002), 32.
37. Pascal, *Pensees*, 132–133.

Chapter Five: Rumors of Angels

1. "New York: Shrine in the Bronx," *TIME*, Nov. 26, 1945.
2. "Angels," *Newsweek*, Dec. 26, 1993.
3. Doreen Virtue, *Angels 101: An Introduction to Connecting, Working, and Healing with the Angels* (Carlsbad: Hay House USA, 2006), vii-viii.
4. Ibid., 49–51.
5. Ibid., 12.
6. Ibid., x.
7. Brad Brevet, "Movie Review: Legion (2010)," accessed Mar. 19, 2012, http://www.imdb.com/news/ni1454109/.
8. Luke 2:10.
9. Gen. 19:16.
10. Lord Byron, "The Destruction of Sennacherib," accessed Mar. 19, 2012, "Poets' Corner," http://www.theotherpages.org/poems/byron01.html.
11. Matt. 28:4.
12. Luke 24:5.
13. Virtue, *Angels 101*, 3.
14. Susan Wise Bauer, *The History of the Ancient World* (New York: W. W. Norton, 2007), 773–776.
15. Frank Morrison, *Who Moved the Stone?* (Grand Rapids: Zondervan, 1971), 69.
16. John 20:10–11.
17. John F. Thornton and Susan B. Varenne, eds., *Faith and Freedom: An Invitation to the Writings of Martin Luther*, 155.
18. Geza Vermes, *The Resurrection* (London: Penguin Books, 2008), 23.
19. Bosley Crowther, "The Bishop's Wife," *The New York Times*, Dec. 10, 1947.
20. Tolkien, *The Fellowship of the Ring*, 69.
21. Ibid., 56.
22. Ibid., 69.
23. "The 100 favourite fictional characters . . . as chosen by 100 literary luminaries," *The Independent*, March 3, 2005.
24. Tolkien–Online, accessed Mar. 19, 2012, http://www.tolkien-online.com.
25. Quoted in David Couchman's *Facing the Challenge* website, "JRR

Tolkien's The Lord of the Rings: The Two Towers," accessed Mar. 19, 2012, http://www.facingthechallenge.org/rings.php.

26. Luke 24:11.

27. C. H. Dodd, *The Founder of Christianity* (New York: MacMillan, 1978), 166.

28. Morrison, *Who Moved the Stone?*, 148.

Chapter Six: A Divine Conspiracy

1. William Shakespeare, *Julius Caesar*, Sarah Hatchuel, ed. (Newburyport: Focus Pub., 2008), 10.

2. Ibid., Act 2, Scene 1.

3. Dan Brown, *The Lost Symbol* (New York: Doubleday, 2009), 492.

4. I have borrowed and adapted a phrase from Sally Lloyd-Jones's wonderful book, *The Jesus Storybook Bible* (Grand Rapids: Zondervan, 2007). In it she refers to God's "Secret Rescue Plan" to describe the redemptive mission of Christ.

5. Ps. 65:5.

6. The phrase "divine conspiracy" comes from the title of Dallas Willard's book *The Divine Conspiracy* (New York: HarperCollins, 1998), and I am indebted to his thinking on the topic.

7. Stephen Eric Bronner, *A Rumor about the Jews* (Oxford: Oxford Univ. Press, 2003), 1–2.

8. Ibid., 19–20.

9. Jonathan Kay, *Among the Truthers: A Journey through America's Growing Conspiracist Underground* (New York: HarperCollins, 2011), xix.

10. Ibid., 190.

11. Michael Shermer, *The Believing Brain* (New York: Henry Holt, 2011), 209.

12. See Joel B. Green, *The Gospel of Luke: The New International Commentary on the New Testament* (Grand Rapids: Eerdmans, 1997), 848.

13. Mark Glancy, *The 39 Steps: A British Film Guide* (London: I. B. Tauris, 2003), 12.

14. Ibid.

15. John Buchan, *The Thirty-Nine Steps* (Mineola: Dover, 1994), 28.

16. Glancy, *The 39 Steps*, 8–17.

17. Churchill, *Memoirs of the Second World War*, 807.

18. Don Lawson, *The French Resistance* (New York: Julian Messner, 1984), 171.

19. SEProductions copyright 2009, accessed Mar. 19, 2012, http://www.beyondcurricula.com/wwii/europeantheater/resistance.html.

20. Both the Hebrew *masiah* and the Greek *Christos* literally mean "anointed" or "anointed one." In using the word "Rescuer," I am referring to the essential mission of the Messiah.

21. Heschel, *God in Search of Man*, 245.

22. Gen. 3:4.

23. I have taken some liberty with the text of Genesis 3:15, which reads: "I will put enmity between you and the woman, and between your offspring and hers; he will crush your head, and you will strike his heel."

24. Ex. 12:13.

25. Ps. 22:16–18

26. Isa. 53:5.

27. Here I am speculating that this was their first encounter with Jesus; the Scripture does not tell us when they first heard him preach.

28. Luke 4:18–19.

29. Luke 4:20.

30. Luke 1:30–33.

31. J. R. R. Tolkien, *The Two Towers* (London: HarperCollins, 2005), 497.

32. W. H. Auden, "At the End of the Quest, Victory," *The New York Times*, Jan. 22, 1956.

Chapter Seven: Our Inconsolable Secret

1. "Top 30 Most Memorable Baseball Moments," accessed Mar. 19, 2012, http://www.prorumors.com/2010/12/rumors/top-30-most-memorable-baseball-moments-6-4.

2. Shirley Povich, "Beyond the Feat, Ripken Fills Gehrig's Shoes," *The Washington Post*, September 8, 1995.

3. C. S. Lewis, *The Weight of Glory* (New York: Simon & Schuster, 1996), 29–30.

4. Dante, *Vita Nuova* (Oxford: Oxford Univ. Press, 1992), 36.

5. Tolkien, *The Fellowship of the Ring*, 239.

6. Anthony J. Podlecki, *The Early Greek Poets and Their Times* (Vancouver: Univ. of British Columbia Press, 1984), 127.

7. James F. McGlew, *Tyranny and Political Culture in Ancient Greece* (Ithaca: Cornell University Press, 1993), 124–156.

8. Thucydides, *The Peloponnesian War*, 91–95.

9. Plato, *The Republic*, translated by Richard W. Sterling and William C. Scott (New York: W.W. Norton, 1985), 117, 123.

10. Fagles' modern translation reads slightly differently from older translations from which I've quoted. See Virgil, *The Aeneid*, translated by Robert Fagles (New York: Penguin, 2006), 210.

11. Lynn Hunt, ed., *The French Revolution and Human Rights: A Brief Documentary History* (Boston: Bedford/St. Martin's, 1996), 77.

12. "United Nations Charter," in *Twenty-Five Plus Human Rights Documents* (New York: Columbia Univ., 2001), 1.

13. C. S. Lewis, *The Weight of Glory*, 36.

14. Plato, *The Republic*, 302–303.

15. J. D. Biersdorfer, "'Star Wars' Fanatics, The Trailer Is With You," *The New York Times*, Nov. 22, 1998.

16. Jacques Barzun, *From Dawn to Decadence* (New York: HarperCollins, 2000), 580.

17. http://nursingstudyguides.net/florence-nightingales-theory/.

18. Mark Bostridge, *Florence Nightengale: The Making of an Icon* (New York: Farrar, Straus, and Giroux, 2008), 138.

19. Thomas A. Desjardin, *Stand Firm Ye Boys From Main: The 20th Main* (New York: Oxford Univ. Press, 1995), 128.

20. Philip Hallie, *Surprised by Goodness*, edited by The Trinity Forum (Washington, DC: The Trinity Forum, 2011), 9–39.

21. Martin Gilbert, *The Righteous* (New York: Henry Holt, 2003), 270.

22. Hallie, *Surprised by Goodness*, 13.

23. Andrew Wilson-Dickson, *The Story of Christian Music: From Gregorian Chant to Black Gospel* (Oxford: Lion Pub., 1992), 96.

24. "Jesu, Joy of Man's Desiring," lyrics by Martin Janus, music by Johann Sebastian Bach, accessed April 2, 2012, www.cyberhymnal.org.

25. Jonathan Israel, *The Dutch Republic* (Oxford: Clarendon Press, 1998), 561.

26. The exhibit was called *Rembrandt and the Face of Jesus*, at the Philadelphia Museum of Art, August 2011.

27. Greg Watts, *Rembrandt* (Oxford: Lion Hudson, 2009), 9.

28. Larry Silver and Shelley Perlove, "Rembrandt's Jesus," in *Rembrandt and the Face of Jesus* (Philadelphia: Philadelphia Museum of Art, 2011), 75.

29. Jer. 23:29.

30. Christine D. Pohl, "Hospitality, a Practice and a Way of Life," *Vision*, spring 2002.

31. Hackett Lewis, *The Age of Enlightenment*, accessed Mar. 19, 2012, http://history-world.org/age_of_enlightenment.htm.

32. Roy Porter, *The Enlightenment* (New York: Palgrave, 2001), 1.
33. John 8:32.

Chapter Eight: Myth Becomes Fact

1. James Steffen, "Rudolph Valentino Profile," accessed Mar. 19, 2012, http://www.tcm.com/this-month/article/133224%7C0/Starring-Rudolph-Valentino.html.
2. Leslie Scott, "Rudolph Valentino," accessed Mar. 19, 2012, http://www.findadeath.com/Deceased/v/Valentino/valentino.htm.
3. Deena Budd, "Rudolph Valentino's Ghost," accessed Mar. 19, 2012, http://www.bellaonline.com/articles/art63110.asp.
4. Steffen, "Rudolph Valentino Profile."
5. Johnson, *A History of Christianity*, 32.
6. Smith, *The World's Religions*, 330.
7. Wright, *The Resurrection of the Son of God*, 80.
8. Joseph Campbell, Betty S. Flowers and Bill D. Moyers, *The Power of Myth* (New York: Anchor, 1991).
9. Wright, *The Resurrection of the Son of God*, 80–81.
10. Ibid.
11. Isa. 25:8.
12. Ps. 16:10–11.
13. Dan. 12:12.
14. George Eldon Ladd, *I Believe in the Resurrection of Jesus* (Grand Rapids: Eerdmans, 1980), 60.
15. I am indebted to John Granger's book, *Looking for God in Harry Potter* (Carol Stream: Saltriver, 2006), for drawing my attention to these themes in Rowling's work.
16. Rachel Falconer, *The Crossover Novel: Contemporary Children's Fiction and Its Adult Readership* (Oxford: Taylor and Francis, 2009), 55.
17. *Harry Potter: The Complete Guide*, Wikimedia Foundation, 329.
18. John 11:25.
19. Mark 5:23.
20. Mark 5:39.
21. Luke 8:51–56. My rhetorical debt to *The Jesus Storybook Bible* is ongoing. See 219–220.
22. These lines are from the 2002 movie, *The Four Feathers*, starring Heath Ledger and Kate Hudson, http://www.imdb.com/title/tt0240510/quotes.

23. Acts 3:15.

24. This imagery was used by Jesus himself, who hinted that the event of his death and resurrection—in which he would be "glorified" before God—was like wheat planted in the ground that produced many seeds. John 12:23–24: "Jesus replied, 'The hour has come for the Son of Man to be glorified. It tell you the truth, unless a kernel of wheat falls to the ground and dies, it remains only a single seed. But if it dies, it produces many seeds.'"

25. See F. F. Bruce, *Jesus and Christian Origins Outside the New Testament* (Grand Rapids: Eerdmans, 1982).

26. C. S. Lewis, *Essay Collection: Faith, Christianity and the Church* (London: HarperCollins, 2000), 141.

27. Wright, *The Resurrection of the Son of God*, 727.

28. Luke 20:36.

29. J. K. Rowling, *Harry Potter and the Deathly Hallows* (New York: Scholastic, 2007), 328. See 1 Cor. 15.26: "The last enemy to be destroyed is death."

Conclusion: The Road Home

1. Watts, *Rembrandt*, 102.

2. John 8:7.

3. John 8:10–11.

4. Sir Edwyn Hoskyns and Noel Davey, *The Riddle of the New Testament* (London: Faber and Faber, 1958), 182.

5. Ezek. 34:27.

6. C. S. Lewis, *Mere Christianity* (San Francisco: HarperCollins, 2001), 65.

7. John 14:2–3.

8. Luke 1:79. Michael Wilcock summarizes Jesus' offer of eternal life, recorded in the gospel of Luke, in this way: "It is offered to all; but it has to be considered by each. It is a universal offer, but it brings a personal challenge." Wilcock, *The Message of Luke*, 48.

9. J. R. R. Tolkien, *The Two Towers* (London: HarperCollins, 2005), 472.

10. Ibid., 486.

11. Lewis, *Mere Christianity*, 65.

Select Bibliography

Adams, Robert M., ed. *Desiderius Erasmus: The Praise of Folly and Other Writings*. New York: W. W. Norton, 1989.

Ali, Ayaan Hirsi. *Infidel*. New York: Free Press, 2007.

Alighieri, Dante. *Vita Nuova*. Oxford: Oxford Univ. Press, 1992.

Aurelius, Marcus. *Meditations*. New York: Alfred A. Knopf, 1992.

Bainton, Roland H. *Here I Stand: A Life of Martin Luther*. New York: Mentor Books, 1977.

Bandy, Mary Lea, and Antonio Monda. *The Hidden God: Film and Faith*. New York: The Museum of Modern Art, 2003.

Bock, Darrell L. *Luke: The NIV Application Commentary*. Grand Rapids: Zondervan, 1996.

Bronner, Stephen Eric. *A Rumor About the Jews*. Oxford: Oxford Univ. Press, 2003.

Bruce, F. F. *New Testament History*. Garden City: Doubleday, 1980.

Buscombe, Edward. *The Searchers*. London: British Film Institute, 2011.

Churchill, Winston S. *Memoirs of the Second World War*. Boston: Houghton Mifflin, 1987.

Cobb, Matthew. *The Resistance: The French Fight Against the Nazis*. London: Pocket Books, 2009.

Coffey, John. *Persecution and Toleration in Protestant England, 1558–1689*. Harlow: Pearson Education Ltd., 2000.

DeWitt, Lloyd. *Rembrandt and the Face of Jesus*. Philadelphia: Philadelphia Museum of Art, 2011.

Dideon, Joan. *The Year of Magical Thinking*. New York: Vintage International, 2005.

Ferris, Timothy. *The Whole Shebang*. New York: Touchstone, 1997.

Gilbert, Martin. *D-Day*. Hoboken: John Wiley & Sons, Inc., 2004.

Gilgamesh. Translated by Stephen Mitchell. New York: Free Press, 2004.

Gisevius, Hans Bernd. *Valkyrie: An Insider's Account of the Plot to Kill Hitler*. Cambridge: De Capo Press, 2009.

Glancy, Mark. *The 39 Steps*. London: I. B. Tauris, 2003.

Green, Joel B. *The Gospel of Luke*. Grand Rapids: William B. Eerdmans, 1997.

Guinness, Os. *God in the Dark: The Assurance of Faith Beyond a Shadow of Doubt*. Wheaton: Crossway Books, 1996.

Guggisberg, Hans R. *Sebastian Castellio, 1515–1563*. Burlington: Ashgate Pub. Co., 2003.

Hengel, Martin. *Crucifixion*. Philadelphia: Fortress Press, 1988.

Heschel, Abraham Joshua. *God in Search of Man: A Philosophy of Judaism*. New York: Farrar, Straus and Giroux, 1983.

James, William. *The Varieties of Religious Experience*. New York: Penguin Books, 1985.

Johnson, Paul. *A History of Christianity*. New York: Penguin Books, 1976.

———. *A History of the Jews*. New York: Harper & Row, 1987.

Kay, Jonathan. *Among the Truthers: A Journey Through America's Growing Conspiracist Underground*. New York: HarperCollins, 2011.

Kingsolver, Barbara. *The Poisonwood Bible*. New York: HarperCollins, 2002.

Krakauer, Jon. *Into the Wild*. New York: Anchor Books, 1997.

Ladd, George Eldon. *I Believe in the Resurrection of Jesus*. Grand Rapids: Eerdmans, 1980.

———. *A Theology of the New Testament*. Grand Rapids: Eerdmans, 1994.

Lewis, C. S. *The Four Loves*. San Diego: Harcourt Brace Jovanovich, 1988.

———. *A Grief Observed*. New York: Bantam Books, 1976.

———. *The Weight of Glory*. New York: Simon & Schuster, 1996.

Marshall, I. Howard. *Luke: Historian & Theologian*. Downers Grove: Intervarsity, 1988.

McCarthy, Cormac. *The Road*. New York: Vintage International, 2006.

Morison, Frank. *Who Moved the Stone?* Grand Rapids: Zondervan, 1971.

Morrow, Lance. *Evil: An Investigation*. New York: Basic Books, 2003.

Norton, John, and Susan Mendus, eds. *John Locke: A Letter Concerning Toleration in Focus*. London: Routledge, 2004.

Olin, John C. *Christian Humanism and the Reformation: Selected Writings of Erasmus*. New York: Fordham Univ. Press, 1987.

Osborne, Roger. *Civilization: A New History of the Western World*. New York: Pegasus Books, 2006.

Pascal, Blaise. *Pensees*. London: Penguin, 1995.

Pelikan, Jaroslav. *Jesus Through the Centuries: His Place in the History of Culture*. New Haven: Yale Univ. Press, 1985.

Percy, Walker. *The Moviegoer*. New York: Vintage International, 1998.

Phillips, J. B. *Ring of Truth: A Translator's Testimony*. Wheaton: Harold Shaw Pub., 1977.

Plato. *The Republic*. Translated by Richard W. Sterling and William C. Scott. New York: W. W. Norton, 1985.

Rowling, J. K. *Harry Potter and the Deathly Hallows*. New York: Scholastic, 2007.

Schulweis, Harold M. *For Those Who Can't Believe: Overcoming the Obstacles to Faith*. New York: HarperCollins, 1994.

Schwartz, Gary. *Rembrandt: His Life, His Paintings*. London: Penguin, 1991.

Shakespeare, William. *Julius Caesar*. Hauppauge: Barron's Educational Series, 2002.

Shermer, Michael. *The Believing Brain*. New York: Henry Holt, 2011.

Smith, Huston. *The World's Religions*. New York: HarperCollins, 1991.

Stokes, Mitch. *Isaac Newton*. Nashville: Thomas Nelson, 2010.

Thucydides. *The Peloponnesian War*. Translated by Martin Hammond. Oxford: Oxford Univ. Press, 2009.

Tolkien, J. R. R. *The Lord of the Rings:* Fiftieth Anniversary One Volume Edition. Boston: Houghton Mifflin, 2005.

Turner, James. *Without God, Without Creed: The Origins of Unbelief in America*. Baltimore: Johns Hopkins Press, 1985.

Vermes, Geza. *The Resurrection*. London: Penguin, 2008.

Virgil. *The Aeneid*. Translated by Robert Fagles. New York: Penguin, 2006.

Watts, Greg. *Rembrandt*. Oxford: Lion Hudson, 2009.

Wenham, David. *The Parables of Jesus*. Downers Grove: InterVarsity, 1989.

Wilcock, Michael. *The Message of Luke*. Downers Grove: InterVarsity, 1979.

Wright, N. T. *The Resurrection of the Son of God*. Minneapolis: Fortress, 2003.

Zagorin, Perez. *How the Idea of Religious Toleration Came to the West*. Princeton: Princeton Univ. Press, 2003.

About the Author

Joseph Loconte, PhD, is an Associate Professor of History at the King's College in New York City, where he teaches Western Civilization and American Foreign Policy. His commentary on international human rights and religious freedom has appeared in the nation's leading media outlets, including the *New York Times*, the *Wall Street Journal*, the *Washington Post*, the *New Republic*, the *Weekly Standard*, and National Public Radio. He is also a regular contributor to the London-based *Standpoint* magazine and Italy's *La Stampa*. Loconte has testified before Congress on international human rights and served as a human rights expert on the 2005 Congressional Task Force on the United Nations. He serves as a senior fellow at the Trinity Forum and an affiliated scholar at the John Jay Institute. A native of Brooklyn, New York, he divides his time between New York City and the Washington, D.C. area.